October 2008

Highway Economic Requirements System (HERS)

Safety Model Assessment and Two-Lane Urban Crash Model

Prepared For:	Federal Highway Administration Office of Legislation and Strategic Planning 400 Seventh Street, S.W. Washington, DC 20590

Prepared By:	Lee Biernbaum Kevin Gay Research and Innovative Technology Administration John A. Volpe National Transportation Systems Center 55 Broadway Cambridge, MA 02142
Principal Investigator	Douglass B. Lee

FINAL REPORT

Acronym List

Acronym	Full Name
AADT	Average Annual Daily Traffic
AASHTO	American Association of State Highway Transportation Officials
AMF	Accident Modification Factors
CODES	Crash Outcome Data Evaluation System
CRF	Crash Reduction Factors
GLM	Generalized Linear Model
HERS	Highway Economic Requirements System
HPMS	Highway Performance Monitoring System
HSIS	Highway Safety Information System
HSM	Highway Safety Manual
IHSDM	Interactive Highway Safety Design Model
MVMT	Million Vehicle Miles Traveled
NHTSA	National Highway Traffic Safety Administration
NB	Negative Binomial
SPF	Safety Performance Functions

Contents

1. Basic Issues in Predicting Crashes

There are many reasons to be concerned with estimating the frequency and social costs of highway accidents, but most reasons are motivated by a desire to minimize these costs to the extent feasible. Competition for scarce resources is a practical necessity, and society seeks to apply those resources where they will do the most good. With highway crashes, given the high costs of mis-prediction in fatalities and injuries, sound information for prioritizing projects with limited funds is essential.

Causes of Highway Accidents

The Highway Economic Requirements System (HERS) model applies crash prediction equations in the context of deciding which kinds of highway improvements are justified for which sections of highway. Thus, it is concerned with the effects of geometric attributes on expected highway accidents.

Driver behavior and vehicle characteristics are also important in determining the cause of accidents (discussed below); HERS modelling does not discount these factors but seeks to identify the causal geometric attributes. The roll of geometric attributes, moreover, is of interest to others besides those choosing among alternative highway investments. Engineers designing highways, communities wanting to reduce the hazard they encounter, and policy makers directing research funding can draw upon knowledge of the contribution of geometric attributes to accidents. Even public programs concerned with reducing driver error and manufacturers trying to build safer vehicles can benefit from being able to diagnose the effects—independent as well as interactive—of geometric properties.

Relationship Between Highway Attributes and Crashes

In the HERS model, only the attributes of the highway sections are used in the determination of the expected safety costs; however, highway attributes are only one category of factors that can combine to produce circumstances that lead to a motor vehicle crash. Crash causes are generally divided into three categories: driver factors, roadway factors, and vehicle factors.[1]

Driver factors involve the actions taken by or the condition of the driver of the motor vehicle, including speeding, violating traffic laws, driving under the influence of alcohol or drugs, inattention, decision errors, and age. Roadway factors that contribute to, or are associated with, crashes include roadway design attributes (e.g., number of lanes, lane width, median width, shoulder width, presence of curves/grades/intersections), roadside hazards (e.g., poles, trees, animals, or embankments adjacent to the road), and roadway conditions (e.g., weather conditions, lighting conditions). Vehicle factors include any vehicle-related failures that may exist in the automobile or design of the vehicle.

---

[1]   GAO (2003), Sabey and Staughton (1975), Treat (1977).

Distribution Among Causes

An obvious question raised in the previous section is, what percentage of crashes result from each of these categories? The body of research specifically focused on the overlapping impacts of vehicle, driver, and highway causal factors is largely composed of two studies completed in the 1970's. Recent research has focused on analyzing the effect of a specific factor(s) (i.e., speeding, alcohol, access control, etc.) in crashes.

According to the 2003 Government Accountability Office report on traffic crash causation:

> One of the most significant studies to date on the factors that contribute to motor vehicle crashes was the Tri-Level Study of the Causes of Traffic Accidents, conducted in the 1970s by the Indiana University at Bloomington Institute for Research in Public Safety. According to NHTSA officials, the Tri-Level study has been the only study in the past 30 years to collect large amounts of on-scene crash causation data. To provide researchers with insight into the factors that contribute to traffic crashes, collision data were collected on three levels, each providing an increasing level of detail, including 13,568 police reported crashes; 2,258 crashes investigated by on-scene technicians; and 420 crashes investigated in depth by a multidisciplinary team. The study assessed causal factors as either definite, probable, or possible. The study found that crashes were caused by human (or driver-based) factors, environmental (roadway or weather-related) factors, or vehicle-related factors.

As shown in Figure 1, driver factors are the primary cause of the largest percentage of motor vehicle crashes, followed by roadway and then vehicle factors.

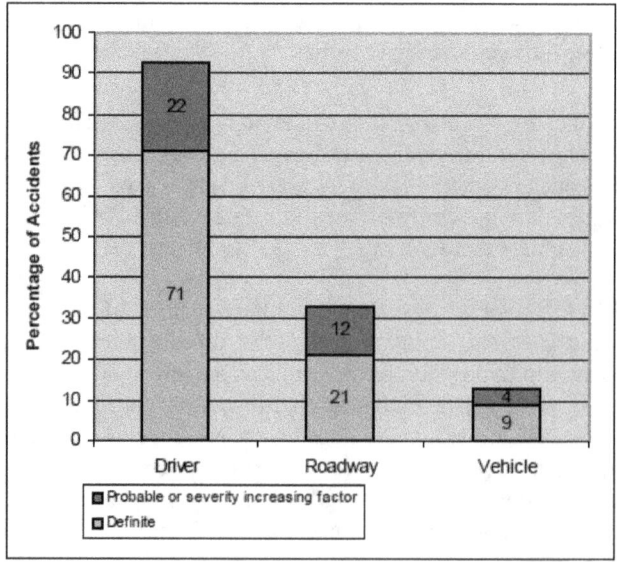

Figure 1. Crash Causes Found by Tri-Level Study

Figure 2 provides a different view of the data from the Tri-Level study.[2] It clearly defines the percentage of crashes due solely to roadway, driver, and vehicle-related factors as well as the percentage of crashes resulting from a combination of these factors. Another similar study was also performed by Sabey & Staughton in Great Britain in the 1970's, and the results (also shown in Figure 2) are very similar to those of the Tri-Level study.

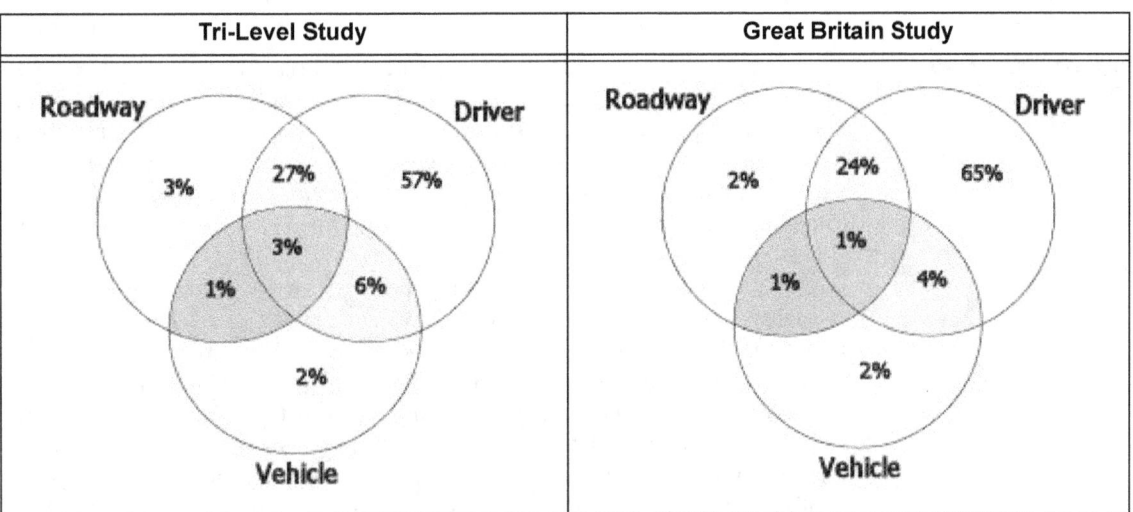

Figure 2. Crash Causation Factors

The most pertinent result from each of these studies is the role that roadway factors play in motor vehicle crashes. In most cases when a crash occurs, a roadway design feature is not the single, definite cause of the crash. Instead, it is generally the behavior of the driver that leads to a crash; however, roadway attributes often play a contributing role in crashes. In fact, in approximately 27-34% of the time roadway factors played at least a partial role leading to the crash.

More recent studies such as the Large Truck Crash Causation Study and the One Hundred-Car Naturalistic Driving Study confirm these general results whereby most crashes are directly attributable to driver behavior, but often in combination with geometric and vehicular factors.[3] Even in instances where the geometry was not the direct cause, identifying *where* the crashes are most likely to happen would be of great use to highway planners.

---

2   Treat (1977).

3   Federal Motor Carrier Safety Administration (2006), Neale *et al.*

Crash Modeling Strategies

Assessing the impact of changes in roadway geometric characteristics is a common problem faced by virtually all federal, state, and local agencies responsible for highway transportation. At this time there are two main approaches that are used to estimate the effects on crashes of making changes to roadway sections.

Effectiveness Rates

Effectiveness rates, a multiplier or a range of multipliers applied to existing crash counts, are a common strategy for predicting the results of roadway improvements and countermeasures. These rates, often calculated from before-and-after studies, can be extremely specific in that they may depend on what the configuration of the roadway was before the improvement as well as the final configuration of the roadway after the improvement.

Given an effectiveness rate, determining the safety cost savings from an improvement is a fairly straightforward task. First, an average number of crashes needs to be determined for the roadway section being modified. Second, the effectiveness rate is multiplied by this average to determine the number of crashes prevented by the improvement. Once the number of crashes is estimated, crash severity averages are used in order to predict the number of fatalities and injuries resulting from those crashes. With the expected number of fatalities and injuries, average costs can be applied which yield the total costs of crashes occurring on a particular section.

Count Models

Count models use regression analysis to directly estimate the number of crashes that are expected on a particular section of the roadway based on the geometric and traffic characteristics of that section. These models are typically developed using large amounts of crash and roadway inventory data, and, unlike effectiveness rates, easily allow multiple changes to a segment's geometry. The most common functional forms for these regression models are Poisson or Negative Binomial, depending on the dispersion of the data. Once the number of crashes is predicted, crash severity averages are used in order to estimate the number of fatalities and injuries resulting from those crashes. With the expected number of fatalities and injuries, average costs can be applied which yield the total costs of crashes occurring on a particular section.

One of the problems with both approaches is that typically the crash prediction and severity calculation are broken up into separate steps. Typically the crash prediction is performed by the regression model, and the severity calculation uses national averages to apportion the crashes into the categories of fatal, injury, and property damage only. From this point, more national averages are used to estimate the actual number of fatalities and injuries. While the national fatality averages are good estimators, national injury averages are no longer published by the Federal Highway Administration in their annual report covering highway usage statistics. Additionally some researchers question the division between crash prediction and severity. While fatality crashes are far too rare to estimate by themselves, some work has been done to estimate property damage only crashes separately from fatality and injury crashes. Multi-level regressions, which seek to simultaneously predict crashes by severity are also gaining traction.

A second concern with this approach is in the actual development of the regression models. The process generally involves identifying a set of variables that are to be evaluated for their statistical significance in explaining the variation in the dependent variable. In general, thorough exploratory data analysis of the independent variables is missing from previous studies.

Interaction Effects

Overall, there has been very little consideration given to the interaction between independent geometry variables. More specifically, cross-product terms are virtually non-existent in most crash prediction models. This is surprising since virtually all research into the causes of crashes generally indicates that multiple factors are associated with the occurrence of a crash. Furthermore, this recommendation was made in a separate report by the FHWA in the early 1990's.[4]

Vehicle Mix

Another example of the lack of preliminary data analysis involves the use of aggregate variables when disaggregate data are available. For example, every crash prediction model has some exposure variable, typically Average Annual Daily Traffic (AADT). While exposure is a necessary variable in any model, not enough consideration is given to more disaggregate exposure variables, such as commercial vehicle AADT and passenger vehicle AADT. Exposure variables are discussed in more detail in the Methodology section below. This approach is also supported by what is known regarding the impact of vehicle mix on crash rates.

Relationships Among Frequency, Severity, and Cost

"Frequency" is the rate at which crashes occur, generally in terms of number per 100-thousand vehicle miles of travel; "severity" is the level of damage with respect to fatalities, injuries, and property damage per incident, while "cost" is the value of the resources used to correct or compensate for the damage.

The expected crash severity (and cost) is not fixed across all crashes. A number of crash factors can affect both crash frequency and crash severity. For example, an increase in volume for a given capacity forces vehicles into closer proximity than at lower volumes, and more crashes occur; higher volume also decreases speed, however, resulting in lower severity and fewer fatalities.

The simplification of modeling crash occurrence and applying a fixed number of fatalities per crash, then, is clearly only an approximation if it is assumed that the two rates are independent. One strategy is to model frequency and severity separately, using the most appropriate variables (such as speed) in each model, with some variables appearing in both the crash frequency and crash severity model. An alternative approach is to model frequency and severity simultaneously.

---

[4] Cirillo (1992).

Summary of Prediction Issues

Various studies over the last 30 years have sought to determine the relationship between driver, vehicle, and roadway causes of vehicle crashes. While roadway geometry is often not the primary cause of a given crash, some road segments experience much higher rates of crash occurrence. As a result, count models to predict crashes provide a tractable option for understanding where crashes happen and the geometric characteristics that can affect crash frequencies. By developing a count model for road segments, highway engineers and planners can reduce the likelihood of a given segment experiencing crashes. These models need to take into account the interactions between geometric characteristics as well as the mix of vehicles on the road. Once a basic model is developed, refinements to that model can include crash severity and cost as well.

2. HERS Crash Estimation Models

HERS is an engineering/economics model designed to estimate investment require-ments for the nation's highways. The model uses an extensive set of data on a sample of highways throughout the nation (Highway Performance Monitoring System (HPMS) Sample data) to conduct project-level benefit-cost analyses of alternative improvements. The model evaluates potential improvements on each sample highway section by comparing construction costs with the benefits accruing to highway users and agencies (i.e., reductions in travel times, vehicle operating costs, safety, etc.) to determine whether an improvement is warranted.[5]

How HERS Estimates Crash Reduction Benefits

To estimate the highway user benefits associated with a particular highway improve-ment, HERS makes extensive use of statistical prediction models. These models cal-culate benefits by using highway geometric design (e.g., number of lanes, median width, presence of curves/grades/intersection) and traffic attributes of the highway section as input to the statistical models, with the output being crashes, travel time, and operating costs. As improvement alternatives are "implemented" in the model, the design attributes of a highway section (i.e., widening a road, adding a lane, etc.) change and the highway user costs change as well.[6]

HERS uses a three-step process to calculate the total safety costs for a particular improvement alternative. The three steps are discussed in further detail in the subse-quent sections. Prior to discussing the models, it is necessary to review the two meth-ods of classifying highway sections that are used by these models.

The most common method of classifying highway sections is to group them accord-ing to the type of service or function they provide. This method assigns each highway section to one of the following general categories, which are known as *functional classes.*

Facility Type and Functional Class

- *Principal Arterials* carry long-distance traffic to/from significant traffic generators

- *Minor Arterials* carry shorter distance traffic to/from lesser traffic gen-erators

- *Collectors (Major & Minor)* carry traffic to/from residential or rural areas to higher functional classes

- *Locals* carry traffic to/from adjacent properties and to higher functional classes

---

[5]   Camus (2000).

[6]   GAO (2000).

The functional class attribute indicates whether the highway section is located in a rural or urban area as well. Figure 3 shows the hierarchy of functional class values, shaded classes are found in HPMS.

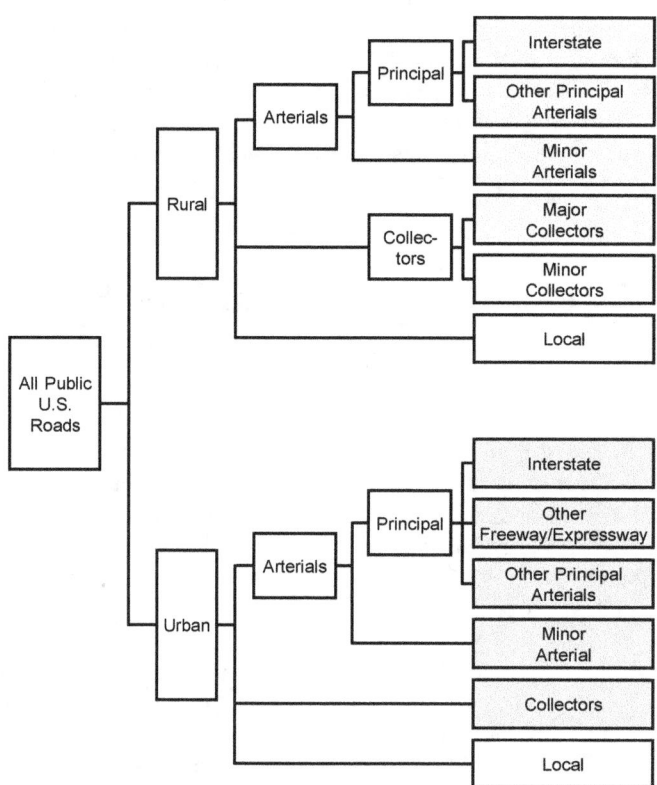

Figure 3. Functional Class Hierarchy

The second method HERS uses to classify highway sections is based on the design attributes of the highway. This method assigns each highway section to one of the following general categories, which are known as *facility types*.

- *Freeways* includes all divided sections with full access control and two or more lanes per direction

- *Multilane sections* includes all sections with two or more lanes per direction that do not meet the criteria for a freeway

- *Two-lane sections* includes all sections with two or fewer total lanes

Severity Distribution

Once the expected crash rate is computed using the crash estimation models, this rate can be converted to the expected number of crashes by multiplying by the number of vehicle miles traveled. At this point it is necessary to estimate the expected number of fatalities and injuries for the section of highway being analyzed. HERS uses fatality and injury rates (fatalities per crash and injuries per crash), which are different for each functional class, to estimate the number of fatalities and injuries for a given highway section. These rates were developed by using national level crash, fatality, and injury data.

Finally, the expected number of fatalities and injuries for the highway section in question are converted to costs. Again HERS uses fixed unit costs (cost/fatality, cost/injury, property damage/crash) to convert the number of fatalities and injuries to an overall safety cost for the particular highway section.

Unit Costs by Severity

While it is important to have safety models that accurately capture the relationships between roadway attributes and crashes, it is also necessary to understand how roadway attributes are affected by the various improvement projects modeled by HERS. Table 1 shows which section attributes can be modified as a part of an improvement project. These represent the potential "knobs" that can be turned within HERS and does not necessarily conform to the list of attributes that will make up the safety model. In the event the prediction model contains attributes not on this list, it might be desirable to modify other component models of HERS and the HPMS data in order to take advantage of this discovery.

Impacts of Highway Improvements on Crash Rates

Table 1. Section attributes potentially affected by an improvement

Section Attribute	Possible Changes
Number of Lanes	increase or no change
Lane Width	meet design standard or no change
Shoulder Type	existing or minimum tolerable condition, or no change
Right Shoulder Width	meet design standard or no change
Pavement Condition	recalculate
Pavement Thickness	recalculate
SN or D	increase or no change
Surface Type	meet design standard
Peak Capacity	recalculate or no change
Median Width	meet design standard or feasible
Median Type	unprotected, none, or no change
Access Control	full or partial
Grades	meet design standard
Curves	meet design standard
Passing Sight Distance	improve to average or no change
Weighted Design Speed	recalculate
Widening Feasibility	lower code or no change

Summary of the HERS Crash Frequency Models

HERS Crash Estimation Models

Six different equations are used by HERS for calculating the expected number crashes per 100 Million Vehicle Miles Traveled (100 MVMT). These different models are based on the facility type and whether the section is in a rural or urban area. A brief overview of each model is provided below.

- *Rural Two-Lane Roads* This method has four composite models (four legged signalized intersections, four- and three-legged intersections with stop control on the minor approach, and non-intersections) that calculate the expected crash rate by decomposing the highway section into sub-sections based on their proximity to an intersection. The output from each of the component models is combined to create the expected crash rate for the complete section. This model, which incorporates over 15 different geometric attributes, was developed for the FHWA using negative binomial regression analyses of crash data from four states.

- *Rural Multilane Roads* This model was also developed using Generalized Linear Model (GLM) regression, and it incorporates 9 geometric attributes.

- *Rural Freeways* This exponential model estimates the crash rate using AADT and lane width as the only input variables.

- *Urban Freeways* This fifth-order polynomial model also uses only AADT and lane width to estimate the crash rate.

- *Urban Multilane Surface Streets* This exponential model uses AADT and the number of signals per mile to estimate the crash rate

- *Urban Two-Lane Streets* This model is log-linear in AADT as was developed by ordinary least squares. This is the least developed of all the HERS crash estimation models.

Table 2 provides a summary of the HERS crash prediction models. The columns in the table describe the original research used to develop the model, the data used to develop the model and the characteristics of the model.

Table 2: Summary of Accident Predictions Models used in HERS

Facility Type	Basis	Data	Model Characteristics
Rural Two-Lane Roads	1998 work by Vogt and Bared, "Accident Models for Two-Lane Rural Roads: Segments and Intersections"	Minnesota (1985-1990) and Washington (1993-1995) data from HSIS was used. This includes 1,300 segments and 700 intersections.	An extended negative binomial model was developed for Non-Intersections. A negative binomial model was developed for: Signalized Intersections, Non-Signalized Intersections, Non-Signalized 3-Legged Intersections, Non-Signalized 4-Legged Intersections.
Rural Multi-Lane Roads	1998 work by Wang, Hughes, and Stewart, "Safety Effects of Cross-Section Design of Rural Four-Lane Highways"	Minnesota (1990) data was used in the model development, with 622 segments over 431 miles.	A count model was developed using a GLM regression.
Rural Freeways	This model was derived from 1992 work by Persuad, "Roadway Safety - A review of the Ontario Experience and Relevant Work Elsewhere."	1987 data provided by the Ministry of Transportation of Ontario.	Persuad's original model was an exponential model with AADT only. Lane width was incorporated by the HERS team resulting in the following model: $$CRASH = 17.64 \cdot AADT^{0.155} \cdot e^{(0.0082(12-LW))}$$
Urban Freeways	This model was derived from 1996 work by Richard Margiotta, "Incorporating Traffic Crash and Incident Information into the Highway Performance Monitoring System Analytical Process."	Aggregate HPMS data was used to develop the original model.	Margiotta's original model was fifth order polynomial with AADT† only. Lane width, was incorporated by the HERS team, resulting in the following model: $$CRASH = 1.54 - 1.203 \cdot ACR + 0.258 \cdot ACR^2$$ $$-0.0000524 \cdot ACR^5 \cdot e^{(0.0082 \cdot (12-LW))}$$
Urban Multi-Lane Surface Streets	This model was derived from 1996 work by Richard Margiotta, "Incorporating Traffic Crash and Incident Information into the Highway Performance Monitoring System Analytical Process". This model, however, used data from the 1994 work by Bowman and Vecellio, "Effect of Urban and Suburban Median Types on Both Vehicular and Pedestrian Safety."	The accident data came from on-site data collection (by video tape) of fifteen arterials in Atlanta, Phoenix, Los Angles, and Pasadena. This data was collected prior to 1994 and included 46.2 miles of urban arterials.	The model is a multiplicative model with AADT and number of signals per mile as the independent variables. The model takes the following form with different variables for a, b, and c depending on the type of section. $$CRASH = a \cdot AADT^b \cdot NSIGPM^c$$
Urban Two-Lane Streets	Model was developed by HERS team.	A table of AADT and Crashes per 100 MVMT was used. The table was populated by HPMS data and HERS crash rates.	The model is an ordinary least squares regression with AADT as the independent variable. $$CRASH = 0.8743 \cdot [-19.6 \cdot \ln AADT + 7.93 \cdot (\ln AADT)^2]$$

†   ACR = AADT divided by two-way hourly capacity

Although the crash frequency prediction models used in HERS were developed ten or more years ago, not much research has occurred since then that would warrant replacing the existing equations with improved versions. Nonetheless, the HERS equations are weak in several respects in light of current ideas on crash modeling:

- *Geometric properties are missing* from many equations that probably should include geometric attributes as explanatory variables, notably the 2-lane 2-way urban streets model that has no geometric attributes at all.

- *Data used to fit some of the equations are thin and perhaps unrepresentative;* models may have been fitted to data from a single state, without testing the model against other data.

- *Changes in crash rates caused by an improvement on a section sometimes are the result of a change in facility type* (e.g., adding lanes or changing access control), leading to a different crash estimation equation. There has been no coordination among the equations, however, to ensure that the differences in the resulting crash rates are a reflection of real safety improvements rather than artifacts of the equations.

- *For some of the models, the methodology and theory* used to design and fit the equations is below current standards for generating crash prediction equations, such that some equations could be improved (at least in the statistical sense) by refitting the equations to the same data.

The six crash models currently employed in HERS create reasonably accurate crash predictions. There remains much room for improvement, however, particularly in the models that do not take into account geometric traits.

3. Highway and Crash Data Sources

In contrast to the limited amount of empirical research on highway crash models that has been reported recently, the amount and quality of data available for crash modeling has been steadily improving. A limited number of such data sets exist at the national and state level, and these are described below.

Highway Attributes

Normally, databases with highway section attributes do not include crashes, and crash databases neither include all sections nor all section attributes. Thus, it becomes necessary to link section and crash databases to be able to use geometric attributes to explain some share of crashes.

Once every two years, the FHWA is required by Congress to publish a status report on the national surface transportation system, known as the "Conditions and Performance" (C&P) report. This biennial report describes the current status and future needs of the road systems in the United States. These reports provide Congress with the information necessary to appropriate funds to individual states for highway maintenance and construction. Originally, these reports were generated through extremely labor intensive special studies, which gathered data from each state, analyzed the highway systems, and then created the reports. In 1978 the FHWA streamlined the process with the creation of the HPMS, standardized the data items required to be collected by each State about its highways (e.g., pavement condition, performance, travel, geometry, etc.), and stored the data for all states in a central repository. This system requires states to report data annually so that the information is kept up-to-date.[7]

Highway Performance Monitoring System (HPMS)

Two types of data are submitted to the HPMS: Universe data and Sample data. The Universe data contain basic highway information (e.g., AADT, Functional Class, Number of Lanes, Pavement Roughness, etc.), which states are required to report for all sections. The Sample is composed of a statistically chosen sample of 10% of all roadways, weighted toward higher functional classes, and omitting local roads (urban and rural) and rural minor collectors. For each highway section in the Sample, an additional set of highway information (48 additional attributes) is collected. These additional data include geometric attributes such as access control, median/shoulder/lane width, curves, grades, and traffic attributes such as speed limit, capacity, K-factor, and percent trucks. Table 3 provides a comparison of the centerline miles and number of sections in the HPMS Universe and Sample aggregated by functional class.[8]

---

[7]   FHWA (2000).

[8]   FHWA (2003).

Table 3. Comparison of Sample and Universe Data (2003)

Functional Class	Sample Miles	Universe Miles	Sample Sections	Universe Sections
Rural Interstate	17,005	32,078	7,333	20,216
Rural Other Principal Arterial	26,076	97,087	10,366	83,201
Rural Minor Arterial	15,269	135,664	5,759	108,923
Rural Major Collector	18,736	424,667	7,340	264,170
Rural Minor Collector	0	267,793	0	5,755
Rural Local	0	2,079,000	0	10,635
Urban Interstate	8,494	14,691	9,159	23,221
Urban Other Freeway and Expressway	4,857	9,930	5,391	16,409
Urban Other Principal Arterials	12,833	57,256	22,283	144,283
Urban Minor Arterial	13,822	94,769	24,340	212,489
Urban Collector	11,687	98,323	21,272	215,811
Urban Local		678,589		6,918
Totals	**128,779**	**3,989,847**	**113,243**	**1,112,031**

The HPMS Sample data are used as the base data for HERS, which provides input to the C&P report. The HPMS data are also used throughout the transportation planning community for research and planning purposes.

While the Sample provides geometric data for input into the HERS crash models, these data cannot be used for assessing the accuracy of the models because neither the Universe nor the Sample HPMS data record the number of crashes occurring on a highway section. Model evaluation and construction depend on matching crash records to geometric attributes of the section. HPMS data might be used for extracting geometric properties not included in an unrelated accident database. To be useful, the crash model must be tied to HPMS data items. In the future revisions to the HPMS database, consideration should be given to adding historical accident data in some way.

Accident Data

Highway Safety Information System (HSIS)

The HSIS, operated by the University of North Carolina Highway Safety Research Center (HSRC) and LENDIS Corporation, under contract with FHWA, is a multistate database that contains crash, roadway inventory, and traffic volume data for a select group of States. The participating States — California, Illinois, Maine, Michigan, Minnesota, North Carolina, Utah and Washington — were selected based on the quality of their data, the range of data available, and their ability to merge data from the various files.[9]

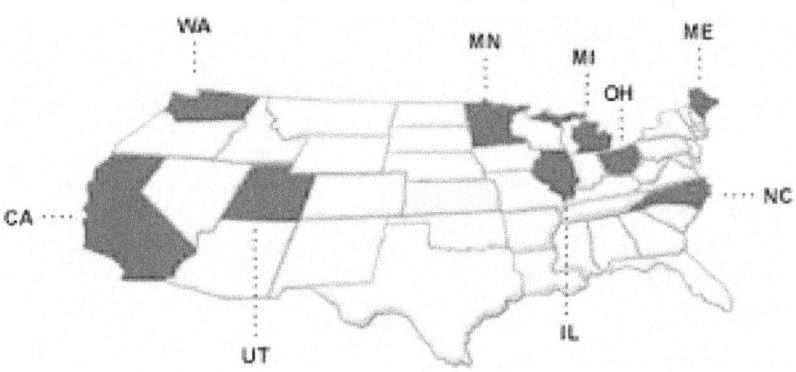

Source: Highway Safety Information System Web Site

Figure 4. HSIS Participating States

Due to contractual obligations with the States, the data in their entirety cannot be distributed; however, subsets of the data are available upon request. Therefore, after reviewing the attributes available for each of the participating States, the data in Table 4 were requested.

Table 4. Requested HSIS Data

State	Years
Ohio	1997 - 1999, 2002-2004
Minnesota	1996 - 1997
California	1996 - 2000
North Carolina	1996 - 1999
Washington	1996, 1999 - 2005
Michigan	1996 - 1997

Data from the other HSIS States were not requested because of the lack of attribute data to support the evaluation of the existing crash estimation model (e.g., no curve data implies the two-lane rural model cannot be evaluated). The subset of attribute data requested was chosen to allow the existing models to be applied to the data, and also to allow some exploratory analysis of the correlation between various geometric attributes and crashes.

The Fatality Analysis Reporting System (FARS) was conceived, designed, and developed by the National Center for Statistics and Analysis (NCSA) of the National Highway Traffic Safety Administration (NHTSA) in 1975 with the following goals:

Fatality Analysis Reporting System

---

9   HSIS (2007).

- to provide an overall measure of highway safety,

- to help identify traffic safety problems, to suggest solutions, and

- to help provide an objective basis to evaluate the effectiveness of motor vehicle safety standards and highway safety programs.

FARS contains data derived from a census of fatal traffic crashes within the 50 States, the District of Columbia, and Puerto Rico. To be included in FARS, a crash must involve a motor vehicle traveling on a roadway customarily open to the public and result in the death of a person (occupant of a vehicle or a non-motorist) within 30 days of the crash.[10]

Currently, the FARS data are not incorporated into this analysis for two major reasons. First, as its name implies, FARS only records crash data where at least one fatality occurs. All injuries and fatalities associated with a fatal crash are recorded in FARS; however, these data are only sufficient to build models predicting fatal crashes since injury crashes are not recorded in this data source. The second issue limiting the usefulness is the lack of roadway geometric attributes. Only a very limited number of geometric attributes are recorded in the FARS data. To address this issue, in 2000, FARS incorporated Geographic Information System (GIS) technology into the data collection system. While this allows the crash data to be linked to other GIS-based data sources (e.g., NHPN/HPMS and state highway inventory database), there is still a significant amount of work required to acquire these data sources and to link the crash data with the roadway inventory data. For these reasons, FARS will not be used to develop statistical crash prediction models. At this point, the only potential use for this data is updating aggregate statistics on the expected number of fatalities by functional class.

General Estimating System

Developed in 1998 by NHTSA, the National Automotive Sampling System General Estimates provides annual national level estimates of motor vehicle crashes and the factors that contribute to those crashes. These estimates are developed from a random sample of about 50,000 police accident reports collected from 400 police jurisdictions in 60 areas. The areas and police jurisdictions are chosen so that they properly reflect geography, roadway mileage, population, and traffic density, and so that the police accident reports can be used to estimate national results. The national level estimates as well as the sample are available for analysis from the National Center for Statistics and Analysis (NCSA).

Crash Outcome Data Evaluation System

Originally conceptualized by NHTSA to report to Congress the benefits of safety belts and motorcycle helmets, the Crash Outcome Data Evaluation System (CODES) is a comprehensive system linking police reported crash data with hospital recorded injury data. Currently, NHTSA has at least partially funded development of these systems in thirty states.

---

[10]   FARS Overview (2004).

Police reports alone do not provide enough information regarding the types and severity of injuries sustained as a result of a motor vehicle crash. By linking police reports to additional data sources (shown in Figure 5), this system provides a wealth of additional outcome data such as:

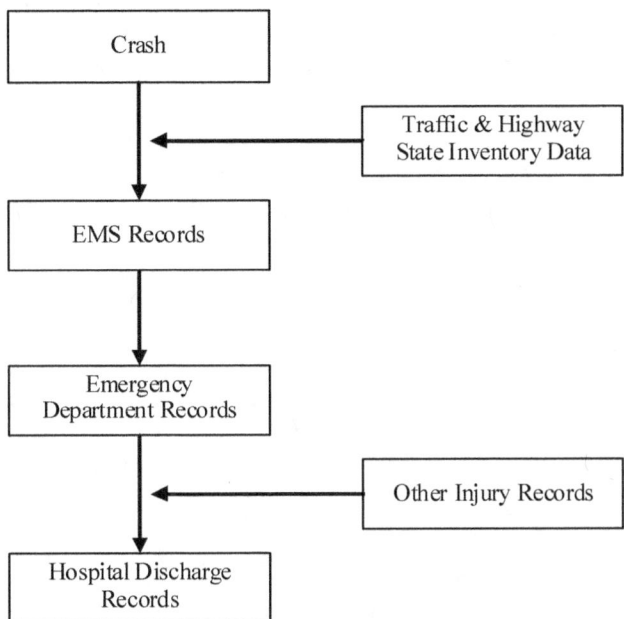

Figure 5. Possible Data Sources for CODES

- *specific type of injury* head, neck, back, lower extremities, etc.

- *severity of injury* requires hospitalization, intensive care, etc.

- *cost of injury* hospital cost of treating injury

- *medical system response* EMS response time, transfer time, hospitalization time, etc.

At this point, just over half of the states have developed CODES, and there is no standardized data model or national level data that can be used for analysis.

Summary of Data Sources

A limited number of data sources can be tapped for highway crash analysis, but the HSIS data developed from state accident sources has developed to the point that rich data sets are available from a handful of states that offer the potential for major improvements in empirical crash estimation models. To the extent that new models reveal relationships among accident characteristics, additional geometric attributes and historical crash data might be added to the HPMS sample sections.

4. Recent Research on Geometric Effects

The primary goal of this review effort is to assess the HERS crash prediction models and develop recommendations for improving these models. In order to assess the existing models it is necessary to understand how the HERS models differ from those being developed through current research efforts elsewhere. It is possible that recent research has developed crash prediction models that are more accurate than those currently utilized by HERS. This field of research has a significant body of previous work as well as a number of recent efforts. This section describes some of the major safety projects currently under development as well as some previous efforts to develop crash prediction models for specific entities.

Previous Research

The American Association of State Highway Transportation Officials (AASHTO) has developed two different tools for state officials in the area of crash prediction models.

AASHTO Tools

User Benefit Analysis for Highways. This manual provides users with guidance for estimating the benefits that accrue to roadway users as the result of roadway improvement projects. One of the sections is devoted to estimating the safety benefits that may result from a highway improvement. This section provides a brief overview of crash prediction methodology and other resources available to a transportation official, including Highway Safety Manual (HSM), Interactive Highway Safety Design Model (IHSDM), SafetyAnalyst, and others. One of the resources discussed in depth is the Roadside Safety Analysis Program (RSAP) that is a companion analytic tool to their Roadside Design Guide.

Roadside Design Guide. First published in 1999, this guide provides users with a synthesis of current information and operating practices related to safety treatments that minimize the likelihood of fatality or serious injury when a driver runs off the road. Developed under NCHRP project 22-9, RSAP allows users to compare the cost-effectiveness of implementing multiple alternative roadside safety improvements. This program estimates accident costs based on roadway and roadside design features.

To estimate the safety impact of roadside improvement projects, RSAP first estimates the number of occurrences of a vehicle departing from the roadway (called encroachments). The second step in the model is to estimate the number of crashes, which are occurrences of a vehicle striking another vehicle or object. The attributes of the roadway (design speed, curves, grades, etc.) are the major inputs to the encroachment and accident models. The accident model also uses the number of encroachments as an input variable. Once the number of accidents is determined, the severities of the accidents are determined through averages and units costs per fatality and injury.

Safety Effectiveness of Highway Design Features

Completed in 1992 this compendium, which was prepared for the FHWA, reports the most probable safety effects of improvements to key highway design features, including:

- Volume I - Access Control
- Volume II - Alignment
- Volume III - Cross Sections
- Volume IV - Intersections
- Volume V - Interchanges
- Volume VI - Pedestrians and Bicyclists.[11]

This compendium was developed as a result of the FHWA implementing one of the 23 recommendations contained in Transportation Research Board Special Report 214, "Designing Safer Roads: Practices for Resurfacing, Restoration, and Rehabilitation."[12] These seven reports are comparable in structure and type of information that will be contained in the HSM (see "Highway Safety Manual" on page 23) chapter on Knowledge, although the HSM will have more recent results.

Current Research

Interactive Highway Safety Design Model

The IHSDM is being developed by the Turner-Fairbank Highway Research Center, which is home to FHWA's Office of Research, Development, and Technology. IHSDM is a suite of decision-support modules (Crash Prediction, Design Consistency, Intersection Review, Policy Review, and Traffic Analysis) for evaluating safety and operational effects of geometric design decisions in the highway design process.[13] It compares existing or proposed highway designs against relevant design policy standards and estimates the expected safety and operational performance of the design.

Crash Prediction Module. The crash prediction module in the IHSDM performs a similar function to that of the HERS crash prediction models. Like the HERS models, the IHSDM crash algorithm estimates the baseline expected crash rate for a highway section based on its geometric design and traffic attributes. In fact, they both use the same statistical model developed by Vogt and Bared in 1998.[14] The generalized IHSDM algorithm, however, augments the statistical base models with a number of additional inputs that are intended to adapt the base estimates according to local safety conditions. The additional steps in the algorithm, which can be applied to any type of crash prediction model, are shown in Figure 6 and are discussed below.

---

[11] Cirillo (1992), Zeeger, Twomey, Heckman, and Hayward (1992), Zeeger and Council (1992), Twomey and Heckman (1992), Kuciemba and Cirillo (1992), Zeeger, Stutts, and Hunter (1992).

[12] "Designing Safer Roads: Practices for Resurfacing, Restoration, and Rehabilitation," (1987).

[13] IHDSM Manual (2004).

[14] Vogt and Bared (1998).

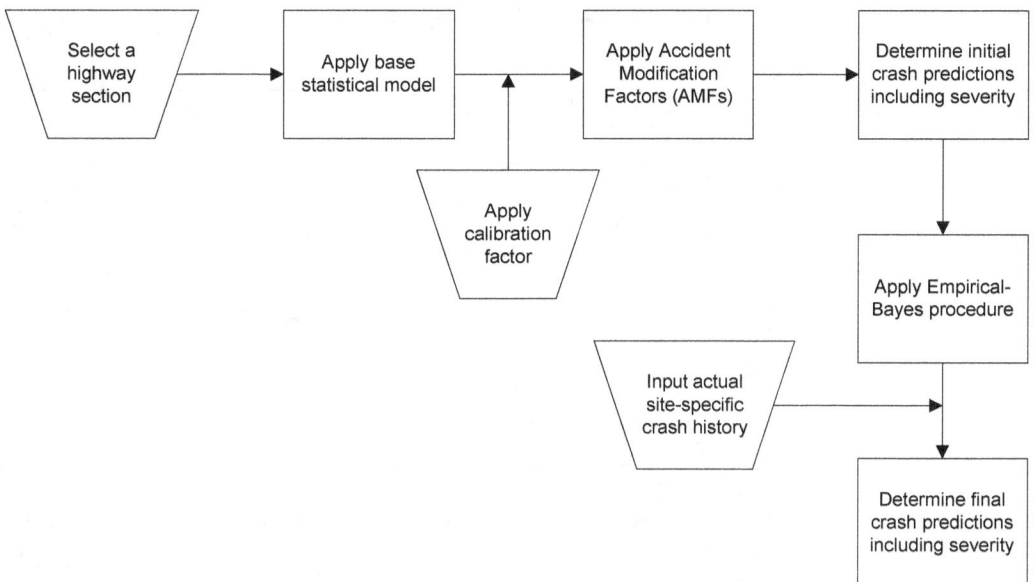

Figure 6. IHSDM Generalized Crash Prediction Algorithm

Since states differ markedly in climate, animal population, driver populations, crash reporting threshold, and crash reporting practices, these variations may result in some states experiencing substantially more reported traffic crashes on rural two-lane highways than others. Once the base statistical models are applied to the highway section data, the results can be calibrated (increased or decreased by a multiplicative factor) by state or local agencies.

The Accident Modification Factors (AMF) (shown in Table 5) adjust the calibrated base model estimates for individual geometric design elements and for traffic control features. The factors are the result of an expert panel review of related research findings and consensus on the best available estimates of quantitative safety effects of each design and traffic control feature.

The final step in the algorithm applies an empirical bayes procedure for weighted averaging of the algorithm estimate with project-specific crash history data. The weights used for the predicted and actual crashes are calculated from the overdispersion parameter of the base statistical model used to estimate the predicted number of crashes.

Table 5. Accident Modification Factors

Roadway Segments	At Grade Intersections
Lane Width	Skew angle
Shoulder Width and Type	Traffic control
Grades	Exclusive left-turn lanes
Driveway Density	Exclusive right-turn lanes
Two-way left-turn lanes	Intersection sight distance
Passing lanes/short four-lane sections	
Roadside design	
Horizontal Curves • length • radius • presence or absence of spiral transitions • superelevation	

SafetyAnalyst

SafetyAnalyst is also a decision-support application being developed through a cooperative effort of the FHWA and thirteen state highway agencies. Unlike the IHSDM, which is applied at the project level, this application is intended to support a system-wide program of site-specific highway safety improvements.[15] SafetyAnalyst is composed of four modules:

- *Network screening* This module will identify highway sites (spot locations as well as highway sections of varying length) that exhibit higher-than-expected crash frequencies, high crash severities, and high proportions of specific crash types.

- *Diagnosis and countermeasure selection* This module will use collision diagrams and crash statistics at a particular site to identify specific safety issues and a set of countermeasures that could mitigate those issues.

- *Economic appraisal and priority ranking* This module will use default and user provided cost data along with crash prediction estimates and countermeasure-specific AMFs to estimate the benefits of a countermeasure for a specific site. These data will be used in the priority ranking algorithm for prioritizing safety improvements at multiple sites throughout the network.

- *Evaluation of implemented improvements* This module will use the Empirical Bayes statistical approach on actual crash and traffic volume data to assess the actual impact of implemented improvements.

Safety Performance Functions. The network screening, economic appraisal and evaluation modules in SafetyAnalyst will use safety performance functions (SPF; also called crash estimation models) to estimate the expected number of crashes at a spe-

---

[15] SafetyAnalyst (2004).

cific site.[16] This estimate, which is adjusted for recent crash history with the Empirical Bayes approach, will be used in the following applications:

- *The network screening module* will compare the observed and expected crash frequencies to identify sites with higher-than-expected crash frequencies.

- *The economic appraisal module* will apply AMFs (i.e., effectiveness rates) for alternative countermeasures to the expected crash frequencies in order to estimate the safety benefits.

- *The evaluation module* will compare the observed crash frequency after the improvement to the observed crash frequency before the improvement in order to assess the actual impact of the improvement.

While the user of SafetyAnalyst will have the option of providing SPFs, a standard set of functions are being developed for this application. An interim version of the SafetyAnalyst application was released in 2006 in order to collect feedback for the final version release in 2008. The interim will contain a complete set of interim SPFs; however, these functions were developed to predict crash frequency using AADT as the only explicit explanatory variable. Different crash prediction models were developed for numerous categories of highway sites, as shown in Table 6.

Neither the categories nor the SPFs are intended to be the final versions, and SPFs with additional explanatory variables will be developed and incorporated into the final version of SafetyAnalyst.

The HSM is a Transportation Research Board initiative to provide the best factual information and tools in a useful and widely accessible form and to facilitate roadway design and operational decisions based upon explicit consideration of their safety consequences.[17] This manual would greatly strengthen the role of safety in road planning, design, maintenance, construction, and operations decision making. The HSM is organized into five parts:

Highway Safety Manual

- *Introduction and Fundamentals* Outlines the purpose and uses of the HSM in addition to discussing the fundamental concepts in safety analysis (e.g., crash counts, SPFs, crash modification factors, etc.)

- *Knowledge* This section outlines the known relationships between safety and highway attributes, including:
  - specific highway design elements (e.g., shoulders, curbs, medians, alignment, and guardrails),
  - operational elements (e.g., speed, rumble strips, signs, lighting, weather, etc.),
  - intersections and interchanges, and
  - special facilities (i.e., grade crossings, work zones, bridges, tunnels, etc.).

---

[16]   Harwood *et al.*, (2004).

[17]   Hughes *et al.*, (2004).

Table 6. Interim SafetyAnalyst SPF Categories

Roadway Sections	Intersections	Ramps
Rural two-lane	Rural three-leg intersections with minor-road STOP control	Rural diamond off-ramps
Rural multilane divided	Rural three-leg intersections with signal control	Rural diamond on-ramps
Rural multilane undivided	Rural four-leg intersections with minor-road STOP control	Rural parclo loop off-ramps
Rural freeway - 4 lanes	Rural four-leg intersections with all-way STOP control	Rural parclo loop on-ramps
Rural freeway - 6+ lanes	Rural four-leg intersections with signal control	Rural free-flow loop off-ramps
Rural freeway within an interchange - 4 lanes	Urban three-leg intersections with minor-road STOP control	Rural free-flow loop on-ramps
Rural freeway within an interchange - 6+ lanes	Urban three-leg intersections with signal control	Rural direct or semidirect connection ramps
Urban two-lane arterials	Urban four-leg intersections with minor-road STOP control	Urban diamond off-ramps
Urban multilane divided	Urban four-leg intersections with all-way STOP control	Urban diamond on-ramps
Urban multilane undivided	Urban four-leg intersections with signal control	Urban parclo loop off-ramps
Urban one-way arterials		Urban parclo loop on-ramps
Urban freeway - 4 lanes		Urban free-flow loop off-ramps
Urban freeway - 6 lanes		Urban free-flow loop on-ramps
Urban freeway - 8+ lanes		Urban direct or semidirect connection ramps
Urban freeway within an interchange - 4 lanes		
Urban freeway within an interchange - 6 lanes		
Urban freeway within an interchange - 8+ lanes		

- *Predictive Methods* This section develops crash prediction models for the following types of roadways:

  - Rural, Two-lane Roads,
  - Rural, Multilane Highways, and
  - Urban and Suburban Arterial Highways.

- *Safety Management of a Roadway System* This section discusses approaches for prioritizing and selecting improvement projects. This follows the same methodology as the SafetyAnalyst application.

- *Safety Evaluation* This section discusses how to measure the actual effectiveness of an implemented improvement.

The first edition of the HSM is scheduled to be completed in 2009; however, a draft chapter on rural, two-lane roads is currently available. The content of the draft chapter has not been fully approved by the project sponsor and is subject to change before the final version is released.

A more recent series of guidebooks to assist state and local agencies in reducing injuries and fatalities in target areas are currently being develop under NCHRP Project 17-18(3). Each guidebook corresponds to one of the 22 key emphasis areas (shown in Table 7) that are outlined in AASHTO's Strategic Highway Safety Plan. Each guidebook contains a general discussion of the problem as well as strategies and countermeasures to address the problem.

Table 7. Elements of AASHTO Strategic Highway Safety Plan

Instituting Graduated Licensing for Younger Drivers	Making Truck Travel Safer
Ensuring Drivers are Fully Licensed and Competent	Increasing Safety Enhancements in Vehicles
Sustaining Proficiency in Older Drivers	Reducing Vehicle-Train Crashes
Curbing Aggressive Driving	Keeping Vehicles on the Roadway
Reducing Impaired Driving	Minimizing the Consequences of Leaving the Road
Keeping Drivers Alert	Improving Design and Operation of Highway Intersections
Increasing Driver Safety Awareness	Reducing Head-on and Across Median Crashes
Increasing Seat Belt Usage and Improving Airbag Awareness	Designing Safer Workzones
Making Walking and Street Crossing Safer	Enhancing Emergency Medical Capabilities to Increase Survivability
Ensuring Safer Bicycle Travel	Improving Information and Strategic Support Systems
Improving Motorcycle Safety and Increasing Motorcycle Awareness	Creating More Effective Processes and Safety Management Systems

Future Research

This section covers some of the in-progress work that will provide results for some of the major safety projects discussed in the previous section.

NCHRP Project 17-25: "Crash Reduction Factors for Traffic Engineering and ITS Improvements"

Crash Reduction Factors

The objective of this project is to develop reliable crash reduction factors (CRFs) for traffic engineering, operations, and ITS improvements. CRFs (also known as accident reduction factors or AMFs) provide a computationally simple and quick way of estimating crash reductions. Many states have a set of CRFs that are used for estimating the safety impacts of various types of engineering improvements, encompassing the areas of signing, alignment, channelization, and other traffic engineering treatments.

Typically, these factors are computed using before-and-after comparisons, although later research has suggested the use of cross-sectional comparisons. The estimated completion date of this effort is February 29, 2008, and the researching agency is the University of North Carolina - Chapel Hill.

Urban Arterials

NCHRP Project 17-26: "Methodology to Predict the Safety Performance of Urban and Suburban Arterials"

The objective of this project is to develop a methodology that predicts the safety performance of non-limited-access urban and suburban arterials and to prepare a chapter on urban and suburban arterials for inclusion in the HSM. This project will analyze the various elements (e.g., lane width, shoulder width, use of curbs) considered in planning, design, and operation of non-limited-access urban and suburban arterials. The estimated completion date of this effort is January 31, 2008, and the researching agency is the Midwest Research Institute.

Rural Multilane Highways

NCHRP Project 17-29: "Methodology to Predict the Safety Performance of Rural Multilane Highways"

The objectives of this research are to develop a methodology to predict the safety performance of rural multilane highways and to prepare a chapter on rural multilane highways for inclusion in the HSM. The methodology will apply to both highway segments and at-grade intersections but does not include full access-control highways. The estimated completion date of this effort is January 31, 2008, and the researching agency is the Texas A&M Research Foundation.

Summary of Recent Research

It should be noted that this section does not include all work relating to highway safety, as this is a large area of research; however, this section is intended to communicate the major direction of the work in this field of research. Based on the information presented here, highway safety research is focused in two major areas: development of improved regression models, and development of improved data regarding countermeasures and their effectiveness.

While there are efforts underway to develop crash prediction models designed for specific geographic areas, facility types, or functional classes, the general direction of the field is toward a more comprehensive process surrounding the estimation of crashes and the effectiveness of any countermeasures. These more comprehensive processes build on base statistical models by incorporating adjustments for recent crash history, state to local level model calibration, and general crash modification factors.

A more comprehensive process for predicting crashes definitely improves the predictive power of the models at the local level; however, it does not add a lot of value for the HERS model. One reason is the lack of national level data required for the additional steps in the crash prediction process. For instance, the HPMS does not require states to submit the actual number of crashes on roadway segments; therefore, empirical-bayes steps cannot be implemented. Furthermore, some steps in the process are not really intended for use at the national level, such as the calibration of the model to local conditions.

Little in the current body of research can be directly integrated in to the HERS models. The crash prediction models developed by SafetyAnalyst are functions of only a single variable, AADT, and the research on crash prediction models is a year or more away from completion. In addition, very little effort is focused on the urban two-lane and urban multi-lane road facility types. This is unfortunate given the fact that the HERS crash prediction functions for these facility types are more in need of updating than the other facility types which are receiving more attention. It is for these reasons that it was deemed necessary to acquire and analyze state inventory and crash data for the purpose of upgrading the urban two-lane crash prediction function currently utilized in the HERS model.

In order to ensure that the needs of the HERS model for crash cost estimation are met, it is essential that the HERS team participate actively in the development of suitable models.

5. Urban Two-Lane Streets

Currently, HERS predicts annual urban two-lane crash rates as a polynomial function of the section's daily traffic, a model form which appears overly simplistic in light of the poor quality of the predictions as well as the purpose of HERS as a safety cost/benefit model for roadway improvements. Yet, a review of published urban two-lane crash prediction studies suggests that crash prediction models for urban two-lane streets have not received a great deal of research. (As one example, a technical memorandum for FHWA's SafetyAnalyst application describes its urban two-lane crash model, also defined strictly in terms of vehicle AADT, as flawed and a necessary research subject.[18]) Thus, an improvement to the quality and usefulness of the HERS urban two-lane street model would also advance the general body of knowledge on geometric effects.

The data explorations and estimation model described in this section suggest that impressive gains in roadway section-level crash prediction accuracy can be realized by considering the *combined effects* of the roadway's geometric features and traffic levels. The first volume in the Safety Effectiveness of Highway Design Features series (Cirillo 1992) paraphrases the results of a series of studies:

> Of importance in the [Cribbins, et al] work was the consistent finding that combinations of geometric and traffic characteristics had a more significant impact on accidents than any single variable and Cribbins et al recommend against further research into the effects of single variables.[19]

Combinations of traffic and roadway geometry are generally absent from published crash models. Capturing these interaction effects does not necessarily require novel or complex statistical methods, though additional complexity is brought in to achieve even better predictions. The model proposed in this section is an example of the GLM technique, in particular the Poisson and negative binomial regressions, the method adopted by Vogt and Bared (1998) for rural two-lane roads. Subject to further validation, this approach could be applied to the entire suite of HERS crash models.

The Current HERS Crash Model

HERS estimates a two-lane urban section's crash rate (annual crashes per 100 MVMT, called CRASH below) as a quadratic function, fit using ordinary least squares regression and then calibrated with a multiplier. The natural log of AADT serves as the lone predictor variable:[20]

The Crash Equation

---

[18] Harwood *et al.,* (2004).

[19] Cirillo (1992).

[20] Camus (2000).

$$CRASH = 0.8743 \cdot [-19.6 \cdot \ln AADT + 7.93 \cdot (\ln AADT)^2] \qquad [1]$$

A literature review uncovered very little in the way of data exploration or other studies that motivated this model. The HERS documentation only alludes to the data used to fit the model, four mean-value data points from noisy data, and provides no reference documenting the development of this model.

Accuracy of the Existing Model

To establish the performance of Equation [1], the current urban two-lane model, the HERS equation was applied to three years (2002-2004) of HSIS Ohio urban two-lane data. (Recall, the Ohio HPMS Sample data does not include crashes.) The HSIS data comprises most of Ohio's urban two-lane section inventory, and includes annual AADT. Consequently, Equation [1] accuracy can be assessed over 17,180 data points, representing over 73,000 accidents. The curve in Figure 7 plots the estimated annual crash rate via Equation [1] against AADT, illustrating the poor fit of the model. The scatterplot offers weak evidence of higher crash rates as AADT increases, a pattern presumed by Equation [1].[21] If anything, the relationship appears negative for the first part of the graph,[22] though this is an artifact of short sections and will be discussed in greater detail in "Effect of Section Length" on page 33.

The poor fit translates into overestimates of Ohio urban two-lane crashes rates (Table 8), and more importantly, mis-characterizes which segments are dangerous. The HERS model predicts 6% more urban two-lane crashes than actually occurred. Figure 8 highlights an obvious flaw in the existing model. The left-hand graph depicts *ln*(AADT), while the right-hand one graphs that same function in terms of untransformed AADT. Both Equation [1] terms translate near-zero daily traffic flows into impossibly high annual crashes rates. This effect becomes more pronounced as AADT approaches zero.[23] Also, the predicted annual crash rate is *negative* for certain low AADT between 1 and 12 vehicles daily (to be precise, $1 < AADT < \exp(19.6 \div 7.93) \approx 11.8$ vehicles per day).

Most critically, the existing equation makes no provision for road attributes and does not allow for a change in the number of crashes that would result from a geometric change. Moreover, a model reflecting particular roadway features in combination might more accurately capture traffic and crash patterns than the existing model. Before describing such a model, the next section discusses how Ohio and Washington HSIS data were analyzed and aggregated in order to provide better insights into the relationship between crashes and roadway geometric attributes.

---

[21] This same exercise was repeated with Washington HSIS data, and the resulting scatterplot is very similar. The graph is omitted for clarity.

[22] Careful observers may note what appear to be smooth convex curves in the data. These artifacts are due to AADT appearing as a component of both axes.

[23] In the HSIS sample used for the model, below, this problem does not have a large effect. Only 67 segments have AADT less than 1,000 and 1 segment below 100. Regardless, these features are, *ceteris paribus*, undesirable.

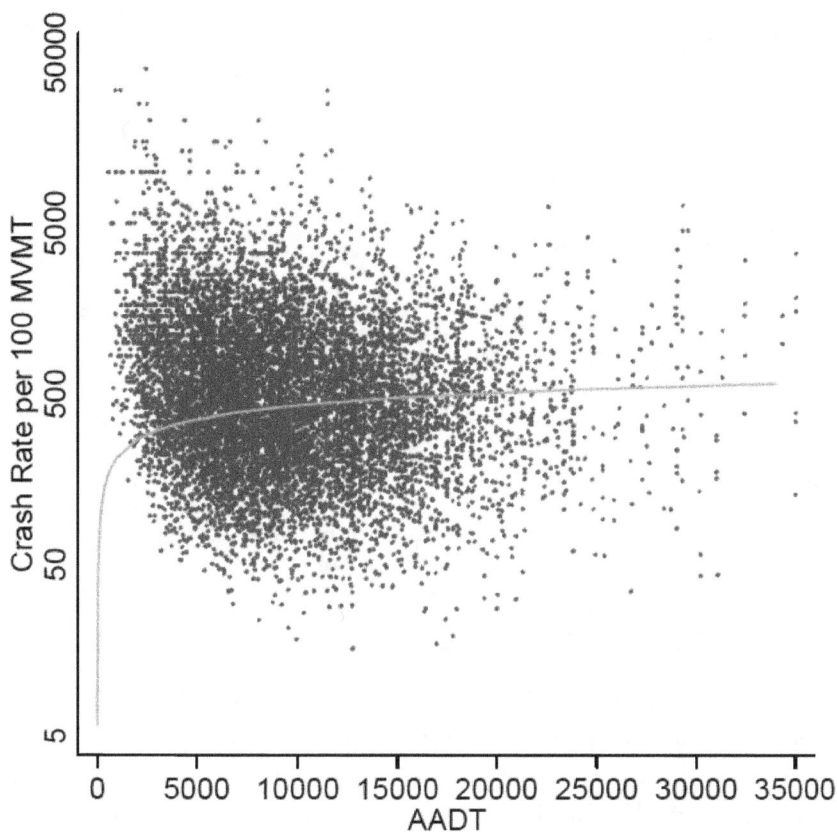

Figure 7. Ohio Two-Lane Road Actual Crash Data

Table 8. HERS Urban two-lane prediction errors (Ohio)

Predicted crashes	Actual crashes	Predicted fatalities	Actual fatalities
77,361	73,038	191	157

Preparing and Cleansing HSIS Data

In any given year, an HSIS state supplies detailed geometry of roadway sections as well as specifics about crashes (exceeding a property damage threshold). A section's geometry is recorded in several data files; typically, there is a data file for the state's entire roadway inventory, another for the location and geometry of intersections, and others describing curves and grades. Files detailing drivers and vehicles involved in each crash are also provided but are not included in this analysis as HPMS does not

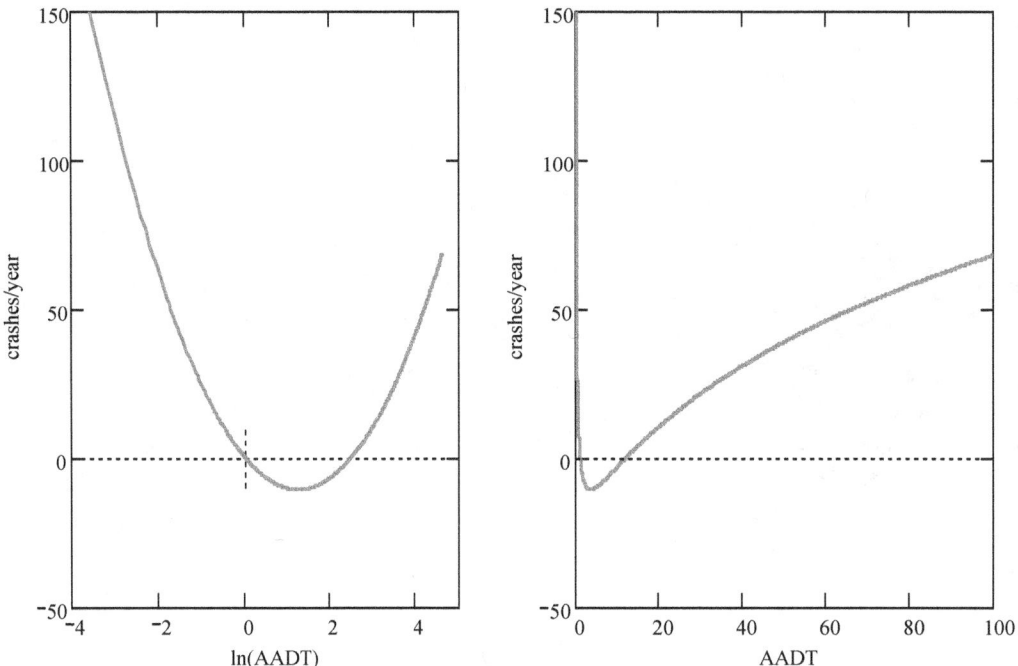

Figure 8. The existing crash equation for urban two-lane streets.

contain comparable information. It is unclear if including such information would change results significantly, especially considering the highly variable quality of the driver and vehicle data and the considerable gains over the existing model possible with a geometry-only specification.

Location of Crashes and Geometric Attributes

Each HSIS roadway section is identified by its county, route number, and beginning and ending mileposts. Every intersection, curve, grade, and crash is identified by its beginning and ending (or spot) mileposts. It is therefore necessary to match curves, grades, intersections, and crashes to the relevant roadway sections. Crashes and intersections, identified by only a single milepost, are simply matched to the road segment containing that milepost. In the event it occurs at the border between segments, the crash or intersection has been assigned to the lower milepost segment. Curves and grades are matched to segments by using the curve or grade's endpoint, again with endpoints on the segment border being assigned to the earlier segment. For each segment, information on curves, grades, intersections, and accidents are aggregated. Details on each variable are outlined in the next section; in general, however, the aggregation consists of the number of curves (grades, intersections, crashes), mean length, and degree of curvature, and mean length and percent grade.

While some models use separate equations for intersection and non-intersection crashes, this method is neither practical nor preferred for two-lane urban roads. First, milepost locations for crashes and intersections may not be recorded in enough detail to properly assign them. Even if such precision was possible, separating the equations would not allow the model to take into account the effects multiple intersections over a short stretch nor the possibilities of the layout of an intersection causing a crash in the area just before or after it.

Each HSIS state has some latitude in how it submits data. For example, the method of reporting shoulder widths varies from state to state. In Ohio, total shoulder widths are included in the data so these are simply averaged between the two sides of the road. For Washington, shoulder widths are reported for both inner and outer shoulders by direction. As this model focuses on two-lane, non-medianed roads with no inner shoulder, the outer shoulder is again averaged between the two directions.

Computation of Non-Inventory Attributes

Lane widths are not reported in the data from Ohio or Washington. As a result, they must be imputed from other information. The total width of the drivable surface is reported for each segment. This may, however, contain on-street parking, bike lanes, or turn lanes.[24] As a result, adjustments have been made, outlined in Table 9, that assume that any segment that would have room for such additional pavement types must also have lanes at least 12 feet wide.

Table 9. Lane Width Adjustment

Surface Width (feet)	Adjusted Lane Width (feet)
20	10
21	10.5
22	11
23	11.5
24 and above	12

The presence of parking is something that would be desirable to include in the model. However, the parking data are frequently unreported (both across and within states) and unreliable when present. Some of these issues have been resolved in more recent years and future evaluations with data collected after 2004 may allow for the inclusion of this important variable.

Sections are defined by the state DOTs for a variety of purposes and with a variety of methods. While segments are "homogeneous" for certain, but not all, traits, they are sometimes further subdivided for reasons suiting the state DOT purposes (e.g., edges of municipal jurisdictions, improvement locations, etc.). Consequently, in Ohio, about 1/3 of the segments in the two-lane urban set are less than or equal to 0.10 miles (n = 5,781) and just over 60% are less than or equal to 0.25 miles (n = 10,766). In Washington, segments often begin at each intersection and so there are many more seg-

Effect of Section Length

---

[24] Merely dividing surface width by two would result in implausibly large lanes as surface widths get as large as 82 feet.

ments. The set contains 18,241 two-lane urban segments, of which 75% are 0.10 mile or less (n = 13,640) and 92% are less than or equal to a quarter mile (n = 16,790) These small segments have two effects, one conceptual and the other empirical.

From a conceptual standpoint, when sections are alike in all geometrical respects, this artifact of section length is undesirable; *a priori*, section length is not a geometric feature that influences crash risk. In fact, with the smallest sections (they are reported as small as 52 ft.), there is a valid argument to be made that in many (non-intersection) cases, the geometric causes of the crash would necessarily be in the segment before the crash. Examining segments this small could lead to fallacious results akin to observing medical patients only in an emergency waiting room and concluding the waiting room itself that lead to the injury.

Overdispersion and Modeling

Empirically, as crash counts are the tallied result of multiple Bernoulli events (i.e. crash vs. no crash), the data are expected to follow a Poisson (or count) distribution. Count data do not exhibit the characteristics of the normal distribution; the dependent variable takes on only integer values, and cannot be less than zero.

The Poisson distribution, however, assumes that mean number of crashes equals the variance. When the variance is greater than the mean, the data are called "overdispersed" and the Poisson distribution no longer is an accurate description of the data. A large number of small segments, oh which, a high proportion exhibit no crashes, can lead to overdispersion. Researchers then seek alternatives to the Poisson distribution, including the Negative Binomial (NB) and "zero inflated" models.

Zero Inflated. Zero inflated models (which can be either Poisson or NB) are two-step processes. In the first step, a logistic regression is run to determine if the segment will have the possibility of crashes. Then, for segments with the possibility of a crash, the number of crashes is estimated. In short, the first step identifies the "inherently safe" segments that represent many of the zeros, while the second stop focuses only on those "inherently dangerous" segments.

However, recent research by Lord, Washington, and Ivan[25] demonstrates that overdispersion can be an artifact of low exposure (particularly in situations with high risk), that is, short segment length in the current example. Lord *et al.* conduct a simulation where overdispersion is reduced merely by combining shorter segments into longer ones, indicating the overdispersion is a result of low exposure, not the presence of "inherently safe" or "inherently unsafe" segments. This also conforms better to the intuition as crashes are highly stochastic events affected by factors other than road layout.[26] In their words:

---

[25] Lord, Washington, and Ivan (2004).

[26] For example, no segment of road is immune to the possibility of a driver having a sudden medical problem that causes the vehicle to run off the road.

[T]he fairly common observance of excess zeros is more a consequence of low exposure and inappropriate time/space scales than an underlying dual state process.[27]

Negative Binomial. The NB model is closely linked to the Poisson model but allows for the variance to be greater than the mean. Specifically, the variance is estimated to be $\mu + \alpha\mu^2$ where α is the overdispersion factor.[28] It is then easy to see that the Poisson is a special case of the NB model, where $\alpha = 0$. Estimates of α are commonly included in NB regression output.

The overdispersion factor can be calculated by running a constant-only negative binomial model. In Ohio, the overdispersion factor is 2.56 and in Washington it is 2.20. As the overdispersion in the HSIS data do not represent any behavioral phenomenon, two methods to mitigate the effects have been employed. First, similar consecutive segments are combined. Second, the NB model (not zero-inflated) is used when performing regressions.

Consecutive roadway sections are combined if each shares traffic levels (both truck and total AADT), lane width, shoulder width, and total surface width. Due to gaps in the data, however, as well as non-homogeneity, many of the small segments could not be combined.

Consolidation of Segments

Overall, the process reduced the total number of segments in Ohio by 4,646 (new n= 12,534) with those 0.25 miles or under now making up under 50% (n= 6,141) of the total. The number of segments under 0.10 miles has been reduced to 21% of segments (n= 2,633). The mean number of crashes is now 5.83, and the overdispersion factor has been reduced from 2.56 to 1.94, a 24.2% improvement.

For Washington, the process reduced the total number of segments by 8,591 (new n = 9,055). Now, 56% of segments are a tenth of a mile or less (n = 5,108) and 79% are 0.25 miles or less (n = 7,150). While there is still a large number of short segments, it is significantly less than before. The mean number of crashes increased to 1.77, reducing the overdispersion factor from 2.20 to 1.81, an improvement of 17.7%.

Since this approach is successful in reducing the artifact of segment length, it will be adopted in future analyses for other states and possibly other roadway functional classes. Adding other explanatory variables to the model will further reduce the overdispersion factor. Many studies in the literature (e.g., Vogt and Bared, 1998) merely discard segments less than 0.1 mile long.

---

[27] Lord, Washington, and Ivan (2004), p. 2.

[28] This particular functional form is sometimes called NEGBIN2 due to the second-order term. Other variations of the negative binomial exist, particularly ones to deal with underdisperson, however the NEGBIN2 form is the most common variant and is usually the model intended when the specific negative binomial function is not specified.

Description of the Data

This section contains information on the structure and distribution of the data. Summary statistics appear in Table 10, and the correlation coefficients between the variables appear in Table 11.[29] The following sections discuss these results in more detail.

Table 10. Mean, Standard Deviation, and Distribution information about the Data in Both States

	mean	sd	min	25th	median	75th	max
# Crashes	4.321	8.403	0.000	0.000	2.000	5.000	191.000
# Curves	0.259	0.930	0.000	0.000	0.000	0.000	28.000
Avg Curve Length in 1/10th miles	0.094	0.351	0.000	0.000	0.000	0.000	9.100
Avg Curve Degree	1.539	7.478	0.000	0.000	0.000	0.000	96.000
# Grades	0.597	1.676	0.000	0.000	0.000	1.000	31.000
Avg Grade Length in 1/10th miles	0.332	1.382	0.000	0.000	0.000	0.100	66.300
Avg Grade Percent	0.641	1.666	0.000	0.000	0.000	0.025	18.000
# Intersections	2.332	3.227	0.000	0.000	1.000	3.000	37.000
Lane Width	11.669	0.633	10.000	12.000	12.000	12.000	12.000
Shoulder Width	3.442	3.195	0.000	0.000	3.000	6.000	20.000
Surface Width	28.736	9.032	16.000	23.000	24.000	34.000	82.000
Speed Limit	39.821	9.413	20.000	35.000	35.000	45.000	60.000
%age Truck Traffic	5.674	4.890	0.000	2.650	4.560	7.670	50.110
Million Vehicle Miles Travelled	1.185	1.799	0.000	0.231	0.550	1.366	22.884

Dependent Variable

The model seeks to explain and predict the *number* of accidents on a given segment of highway. As a count, it is bounded by zero from below and takes on only integer values. Moreover, a large number of sections exhibit zero crashes in any given year. Consequently, the normal distribution should neither be expected in either the number of crashes nor in the error structure predicting such crashes. As seen in Figure 9, there are many segments with zero crashes and progressively fewer as the number of crashes increases, with the maximum at 191 crashes. Also evident is that the distribution is not quite Poisson (it is overdispersed, as discussed above), and so NB methods will be used instead.[30]

Independent Variables

Million Vehicle Miles Travelled (MVMT). In order to adjust for the difference in exposure (section length and traffic volume) each segment has to accidents, MVMT is included in the model.[31] MVMT is computed as seen in Equation [2] and then the natural log was taken. Unsurprisingly, MVMT has a positive correlation with crashes

---

[29] These summary data are tabulated by state in "Appendix 2: State-level Statistics" on page 81.

[30] See "Modeling Methodology" on page 48.

[31] Mathematically, there is no difference between including AADT and segment length as separate variables or combined into one. In either case, the variables represent the exposure to crashes, rather than a geometric characteristic, and need to be included only to "mop up" the explanatory value due to them

	# Crash	# Curves	Avg Curve Length	Avg Curve Degree	# Grades	Avg Grade Length	Avg % Grade	# I-sect	Lane Width	Shldr Width	Surf Width	Speed Limit	%age Truck Traffic	ln MVMT
# Crashes	1.000													
# Curves	0.037	1.000												
Avg Curve Length	-0.035	0.370	1.000											
Avg Curve Degree	-0.005	0.339	0.152	1.000										
# Grades	0.022	0.358	0.165	0.073	1.000									
Avg Grade Length	-0.029	0.151	0.158	0.028	0.187	1.000								
Avg % Grade	0.030	0.245	0.132	0.129	0.355	0.277	1.000							
# Intersections	0.478	0.113	-0.021	0.056	0.076	-0.031	0.129	1.000						
Lane Width	0.050	-0.125	-0.032	-0.065	-0.071	-0.022	-0.096	-0.023	1.000					
Shoulder Width	-0.100	0.054	0.127	-0.027	0.075	0.083	0.023	-0.089	-0.152	1.000				
Surface Width	0.054	-0.137	-0.094	-0.047	-0.087	-0.065	-0.111	-0.053	0.453	-0.460	1.000			
Speed Limit	-0.077	0.101	0.119	-0.009	0.081	0.082	0.069	-0.034	-0.167	0.441	-0.358	1.000		
%age Truck Traffic	-0.084	-0.037	0.008	-0.043	0.001	0.026	-0.049	-0.066	0.057	0.130	-0.031	0.181	1.000	
ln MVMT	0.644	0.170	0.072	0.002	0.229	0.041	0.114	0.540	-0.022	0.092	-0.137	0.126	-0.047	1.000

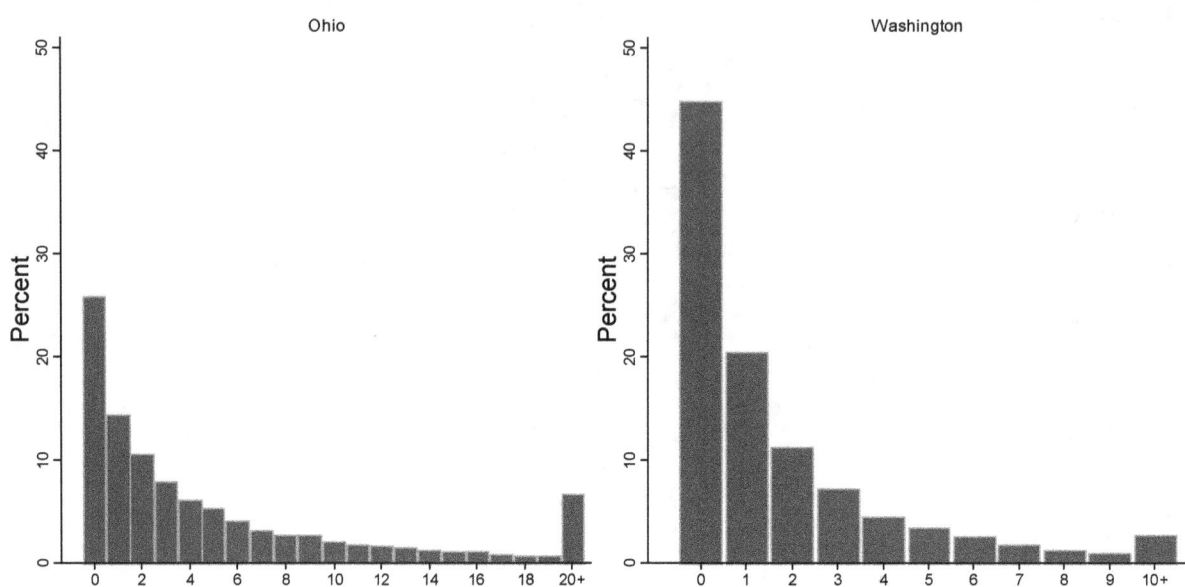

Figure 9. Number of Crashes Per Segment in Ohio and Washington

(Ohio r^2 = 0.66, Washington r^2 = 0.52). MVMT ranges from 0.0004 to 22.8841 in Ohio and 0.0028 to 20.2584 in Washington. The Ohio mean is 1.41 with 60% of observations occurring below 1.0 and 98% below 10.0; in Washington, the mean is 0.83 with 77% of observations below 1.0, 97.8% below 5.0, and 99.7% below 10.0.

While MVMT does not represent specific geometry, it is included as a type of exposure variable to "mop up" the explanatory value due to the increased ability for a longer (or more heavily used) segment to contain crashes. While the coefficient on MVMT will not be constrained to 1.0, the concept will be imitated by taking the natural log of MVMT. [32] Doing this also allows practitioners to interpret the eventual model coefficients as an elasticity. The distribution of ln(MVMT) is shown in Figure 10.

$$\text{MVMT} = \frac{\text{AADT} \times 365 \times \text{Segment Length}}{1,000,000} \qquad [2]$$

Number of Grades. The mean number of grades seen across Ohio observations is 0.23 with over 87% of segments having no grade at all.[33] A "new" grade is recorded any time the direction or degree of grade changes. When considering only segments that have one or more grades (n = 1,544), the mean is 1.84 and more than 60% of

---

[32] There is no reason to believe, *a priori*, that crashes increase at the same rate as MVMT increases. That is, the traditional exposure procedure constrains the elasticity to 1.0, while this model will not constrain the relationship to unit elasticity.

[33] In Ohio, grades only enter the data set when greater than 3%.

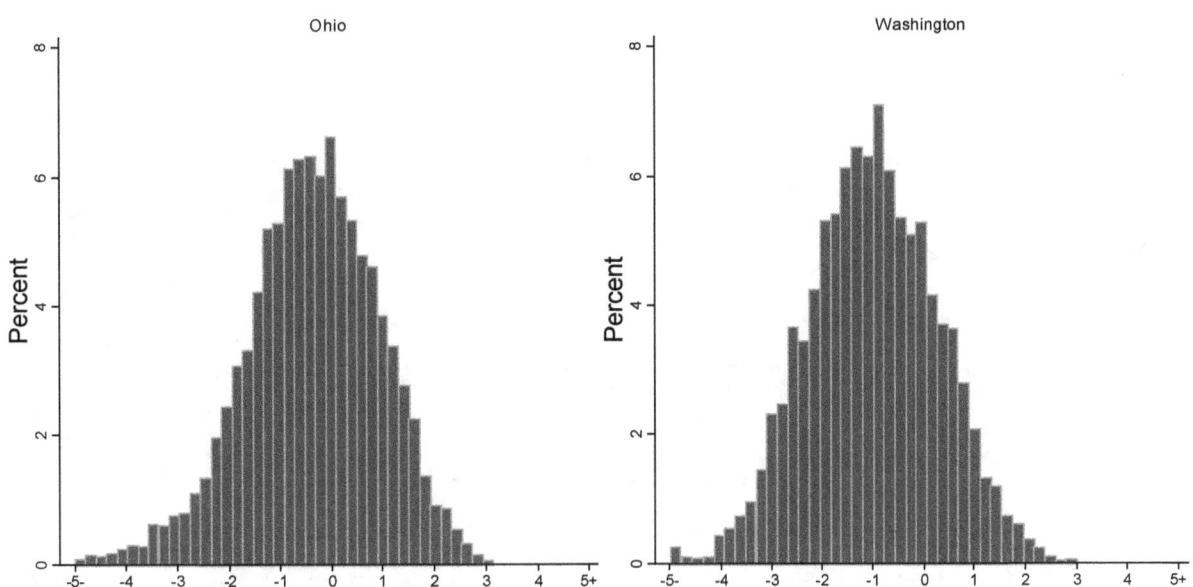

Figure 10. Natural Log of MVMT

these segments have only one grade. The maximum number of grades is 15, seen in 3 segments. In Washington, the mean number of grades is 1.16 but of the 4,298 segments with a grade, the mean is 2.45 and more than 50% of these segments have only one grade. The maximum number of grades is 31, seen in 5 segments.

Crashes are expected to increase with the number of grades in a segment. This is supported by the boxplots in Figure 11 and the (small) positive computed correlation (Ohio r^2 = 0.10, Washington r^2 = 0.31) between the number of grades and crashes. Note that the small dots are outliers (beyond 1.5 times the Inter-Quartile Range) and the plus sign represents the median.

Number of Curves. Characterization of the number of curves is similar to the number of grades, though with even fewer cases. The number of curves range from 0 (>90%) to 19 in Ohio[34] and from 0 (>75%) to 28 in Washington. The mean within Ohio segments is 0.19 curves per segment and 1.89 in segments that possess one or more curves (n = 1,250). In Washington, the mean is 0.35 curves per segment and 1.49 in segments that possess one or more curves (n = 2,125).

Like grades, crashes are expected to increase with number of curves, though the possibility that drivers are more careful on curviest roads should be considered. The correlation coefficient is weak at 0.05 (Ohio) and 0.14 (Washington). Figure 12 shows this relationship.

---

[34] Again, curves of less than 3 degrees do not appear to be fully included in the file.

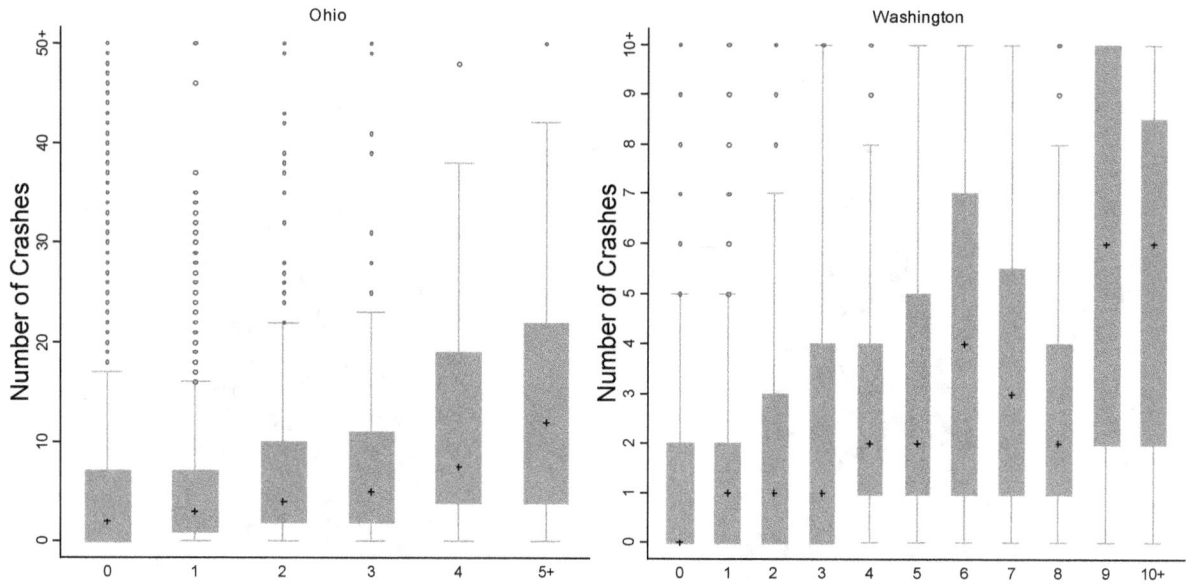

Figure 11. Crashes by Number of Grades

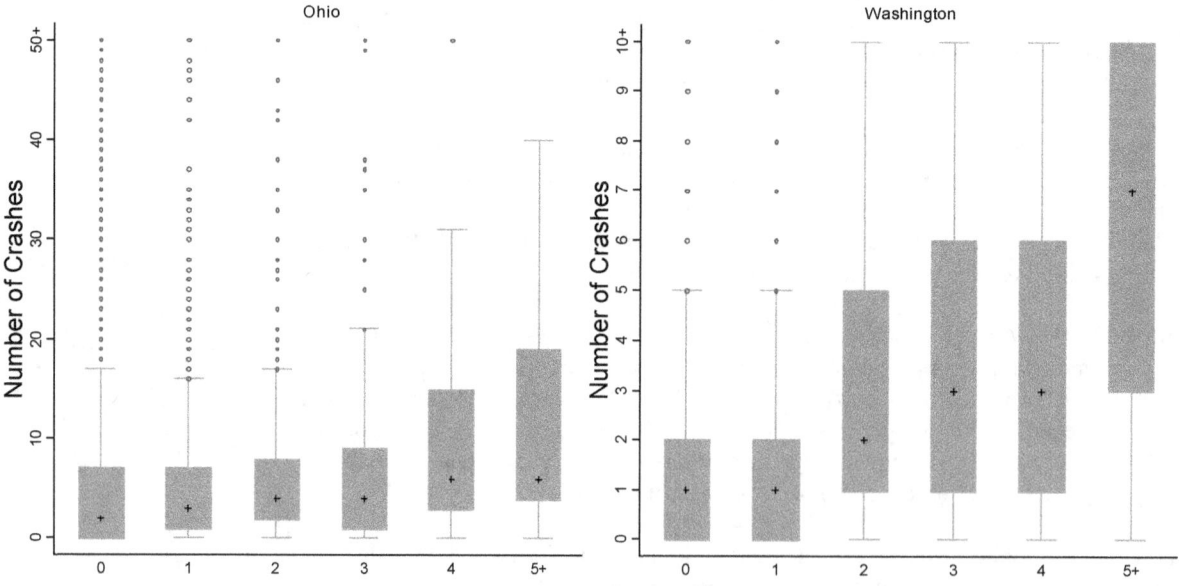

Figure 12. Crashes by Number of Curves

Number of Intersections. Like curves and grades, intersections are expected to be correlated with more crashes. Over 80% of Ohio segments contain at least one intersection with a mean value of 3.16 for all segments and 3.82 among segments with at least one intersection (n = 10,380). Two segments contain 37 intersections, though, as seen in Figure 13, 90% of segments have seven intersections or less. Unlike Ohio,

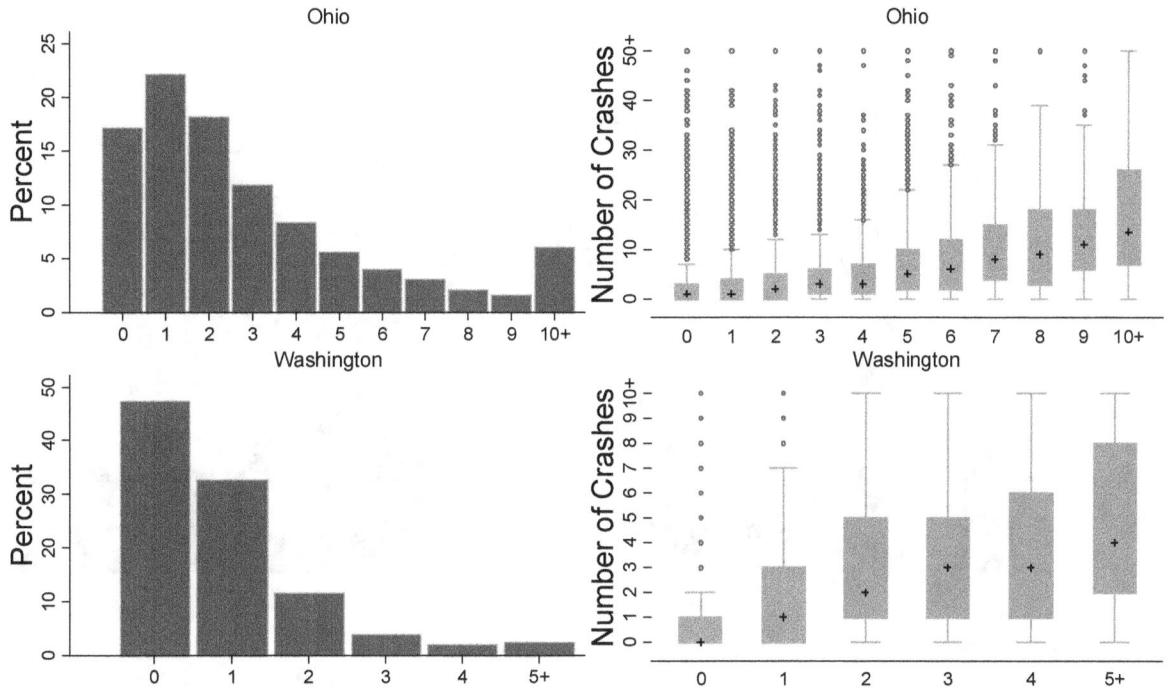

Figure 13. Intersections per Segment (Left) and Crashes by Number of Intersections (Right)

only 53% of Washington segments contain at least one intersection (see Figure 13). The mean is 0.94 for all segments and 1.78 among segments with at least one intersection (n = 4,762). Eight segments contain 20 intersections but the overwhelming majority (>95%) of segments have three intersections or less. Unsurprisingly, the number of intersections is positively correlated with accidents (Ohio $r^2 = 0.44$, Washington $r^2 = 0.49$), which shows in the figures.

There is a moderate correlation between the number of curves, grades, and intersections (0.19 - 0.38 for each pair in both states) which could imply that segments may be defined in such a way as to put multiple pieces of augmenting geometry into the same segment.

Speed Limit. While there is expected to be a link between higher speeds and more crashes (due to reduced reaction time), that link may not necessarily hold when the measure is *speed limit* rather than actual speed. In fact, accidents are likely correlated with the number of people who *exceed* the posted speed limits, particularly on curvy roads or those with limited visibility. Moreover, the speeds travelled at intersections may be significantly lower than posted speeds due to the presence of stop lights or signs. As such, the expected link with crashes is small, and is verified by the data, where $r^2 = -0.07$. Speed limits range from 20 - 55 mph in Ohio and 25 - 60 mph in Washington with a mean of 39.8 mph in both states.

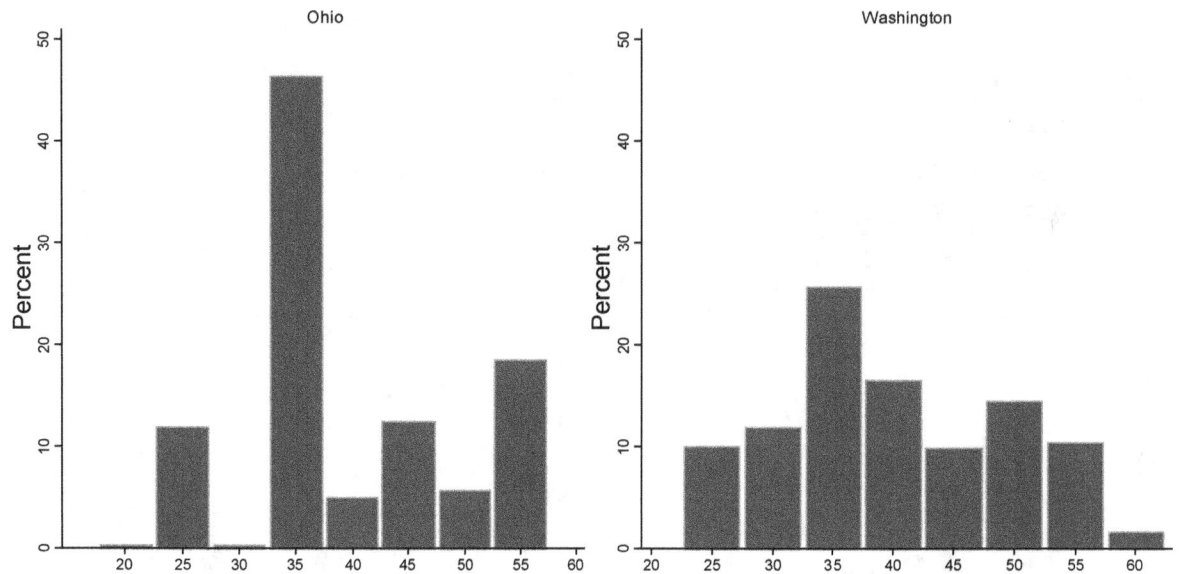

Figure 14. Speed Limits (mph)

Lane width. Narrow lane width can be expected to be positively correlated with crashes as narrow lanes would increase the possibility of contact with vehicles travelling in the opposite direction or with stationary objects on the side of the road, though again, drivers may be more attentive when driving in particularly narrow lanes. However, 78% and 72% of Ohio and Washington segments, respectively, have lane widths of 12 feet, as seen in Figure 15.[35] The lack of variation in the data could lead to difficulty in finding useful or significant results with this variable. The correlation with crash counts is quite low ($r^2 = 0.08$ in Ohio and $r^2 = -0.07$ in Washington).

Shoulder Width. Shoulder width can affect crash rates through their ability to serve as a breakdown lane (or not, and thus lead to obstacles in the road), by providing room to swerve from a danger in the road, and by providing a buffer from roadside obstacles. Particularly in urban environments, however, shoulders may serve as street-side parking and thus increase the possibility for crashes with vehicles entering and leaving the through lanes. Shoulder widths range from 0 feet (36% of segments) to 15 feet (2 segments) with a mean of 3.06 feet in Ohio. In Washington, shoulder

---

[35] See discussion above on the determination of lane widths.

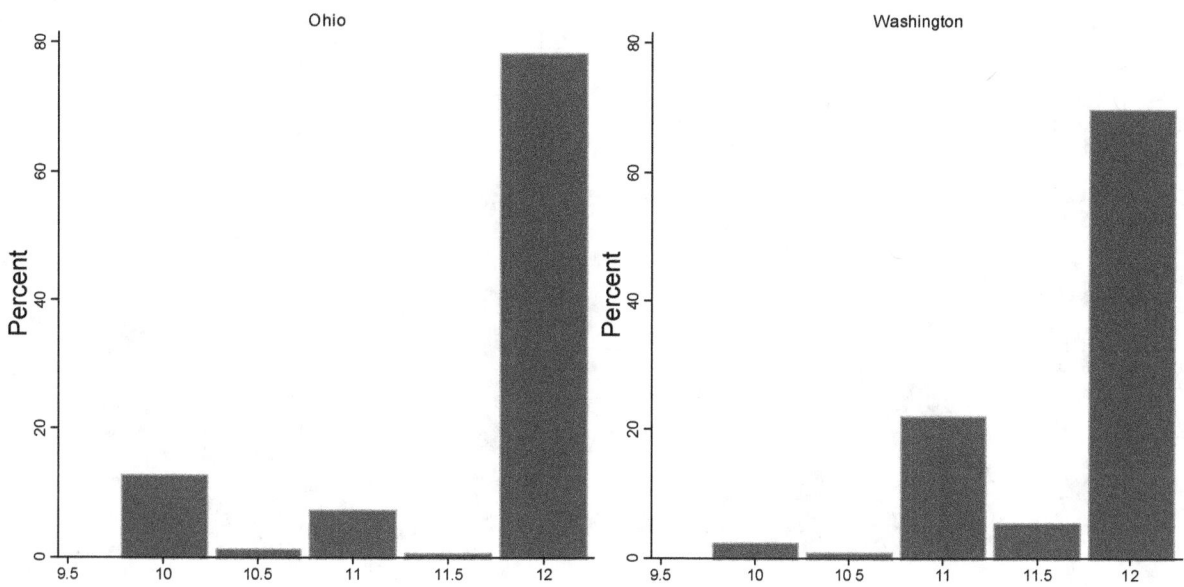

Figure 15. Lane Widths (ft)

widths range from 0 feet (29% of segments) to 20 feet (3 segments) with a mean of 4.08 feet. As seen in Figure 16, shoulder widths are clustered at 0, 2-4, 6, and 8 feet. Shoulder width has no correlation with crashes (Ohio r^2 = -0.10, Washington r^2 = 0.02). It also has a relatively high correlation with speed limits (r^2 = 0.43 in Ohio, r^2= 0.52 in Washington), a positive correlation with truck traffic levels, and the length of curves, but very weak correlations with other information about curves. In Washington, correlations with grade length and percent are moderate as well.

Truck Percentage. The volume of traffic on a given road segment has, of course, a strong possibility of affecting the number of crashes on the segment (at the least, it provides an upper bound). While total traffic is represented in the model as the ln(MVMT) variable, it is plausible that truck traffic fundamentally differs in the number and types of crashes a segment sees.[36] In practice, however, truck percentage has a negative, but weak (Ohio r^2 = -0.09, Washington r^2 = -0.06), correlation with accident counts. Truck traffic is fairly low with mean segments having 5%-6% of traffic in trucks pass through each day and a maximum value of just over 50% in Ohio and 40% in Washington. The distribution of truck percentage can be seen in Figure 17.

---

[36] Moreover, there could be variation in types of trucks (local delivery vs. heavy goods vs. drayage trucks, etc.); the HSIS data, however, do not contain enough information to determine the truck mix.

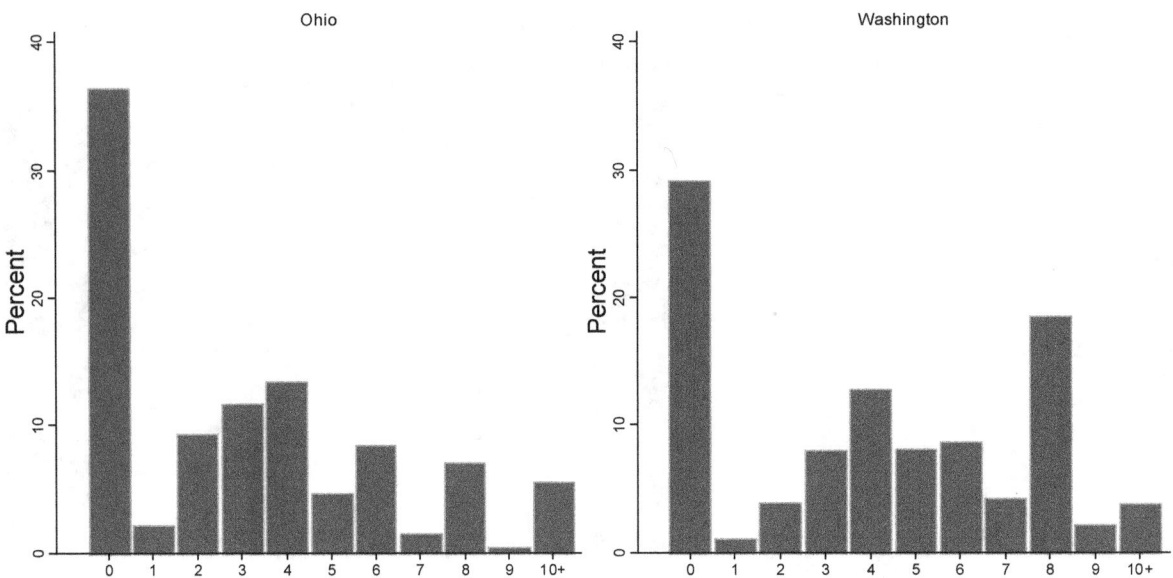

Figure 16. Shoulder Widths (ft)

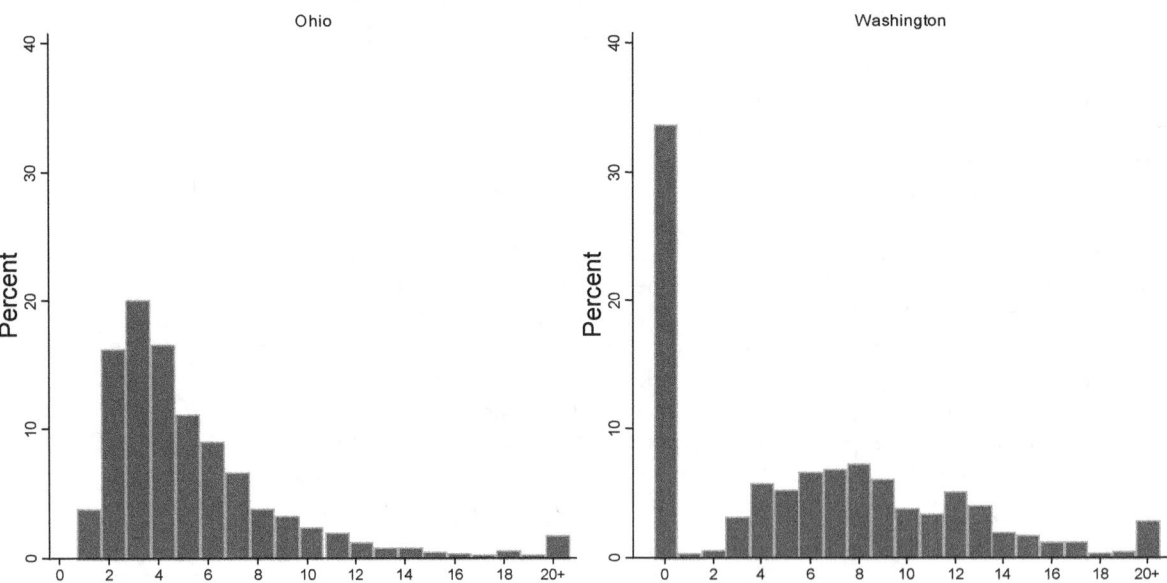

Figure 17. Percentage of Truck Traffic

Average Curve Length. In Ohio, the average curve length is 0.005 miles (26 feet). This number is heavily weighted by the fact that over 90% of segments have zero curves. Among segments with a curve, the average length is 0.05 miles (260 feet), with a range of 0.003 miles (16 feet) to 0.35 miles. In Washington, the average length is 0.017 miles (90 feet) but when excluding the 75% of segments with no curves, the average length is 0.07 miles (37 feet), with a range of 0.002 to 0.91 miles (11 to 4800 feet). The correlation between curve length and crashes is essentially non-existent in both states, but for segments with at least one curve, it is -0.04 in Ohio and -0.13 in Washington, indicating a possible break point. The distribution of curve lengths (for segments with more than one curve) is shown in Figure 18.[37]

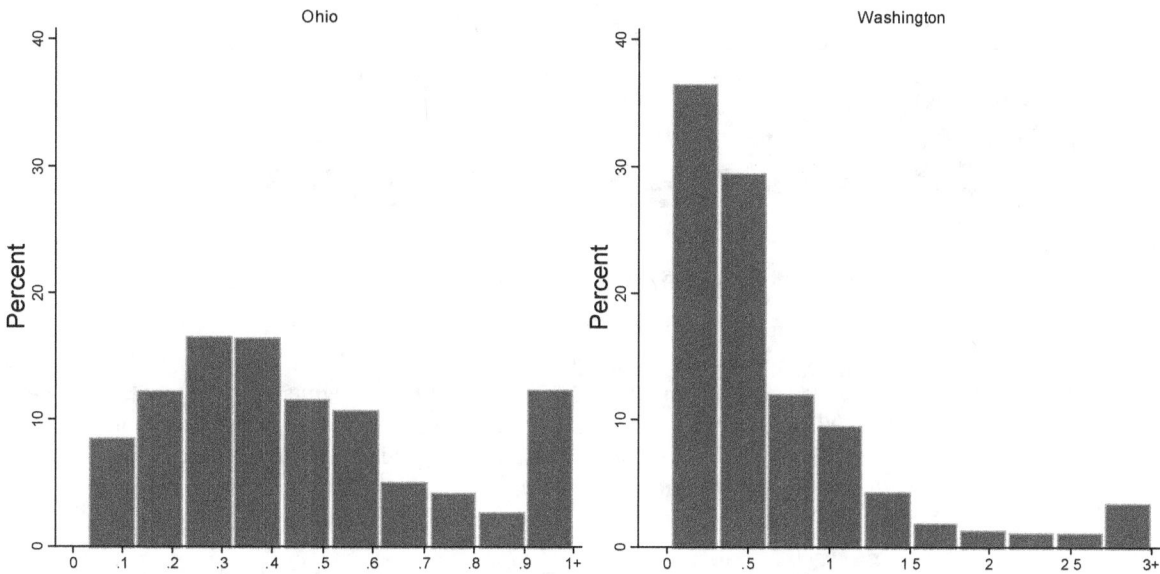

Figure 18. Average Curve Length (0.10 miles)

Average Curve Degree. The average degree of curvature across Ohio segments is 1.67 degrees, but of the 1,250 segments with at least one curve, the average is 16.74 with a range of 0.29 to 96 degrees. In Washington, the overall average is 1.32 degrees, but ranges from 0.06 to 80 degrees. In the 1,813 segments with at least one curve, the mean is 5.38 degrees. The correlation between curve degree and crash counts is low in both states with r^2 = -0.01 (Ohio) and r^2 = 0.01 (Washington) but among segments with a curve, the correlations are r2 = -0.11 (Ohio) and r^2 = -0.08 (Washington). A histogram of (non-zero) curve degrees is in Figure 19.

Average Grade Length. Across Ohio segments, the mean length of a grade is 0.014 miles (74 feet). Of the 12% of segments with a grade, the mean length is 0.111 miles (586 feet). The shortest average grade is 0.005 miles (26 feet) while the longest

---

[37] Grade and Curve length are represented in graphs and the model equations in 1/10th miles.

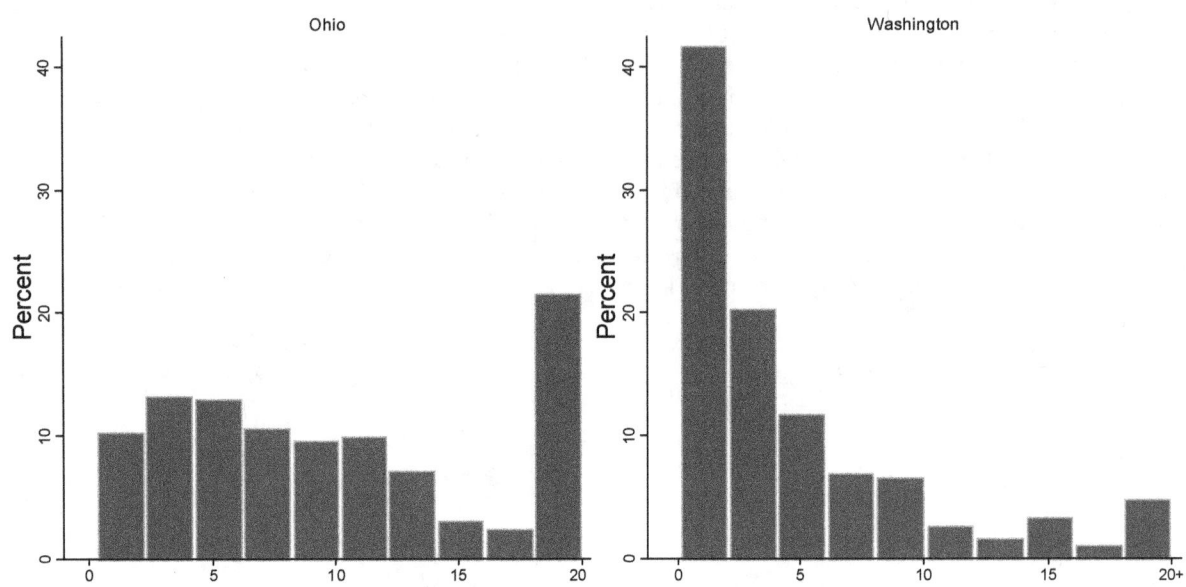

Figure 19. Average Curve Degree

is 1.83 miles.[38] In Washington, the average is 0.066 miles (350 feet) across all segments and 0.137 miles (720 feet) in the 49% of segments with a grade, ranging from 0.003 (16 feet) to 6.63 miles. A histogram of grade lengths greater than zero appears in Figure 20.[39] The correlation between grade length and crash counts, however, is small at $r^2 = 0.03$ and $r^2 = 0.02$ in Ohio and Washington, respectively, and stays small when considering only segments possessing grades.

Average Percent Grade. The mean percent grade is 0.633 across Ohio segments and 5.135 percent for the segments with at least one grade. In Washington, the overall mean is 0.655 percent and 1.36 percent in segments with grades. They range from 0.286 to 18 percent in Ohio and 0.003 to 10 percent in Washington, as shown in Figure 21. The correlation with crashes is also very small for all segments and for segments with at least one grade.

---

[38] Recall that the variable is the average length of the grade aggregated across all grades that end in the segment.

[39] Grade and Curve length are represented in graphs and the model equations in 1/10th miles.

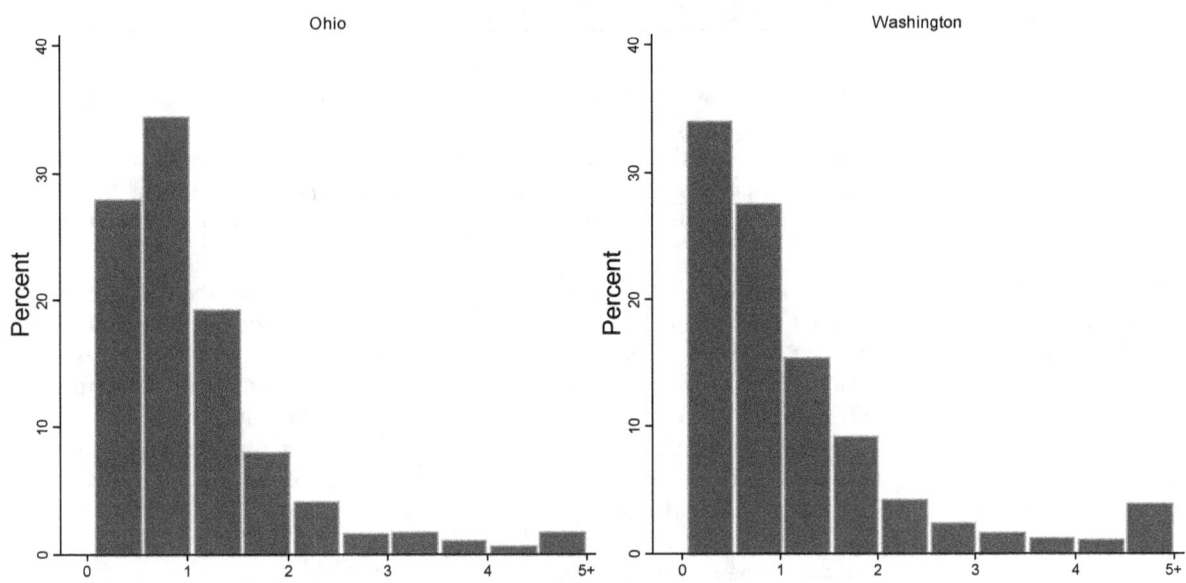

Figure 20. Average Grade Length (0.10 miles)

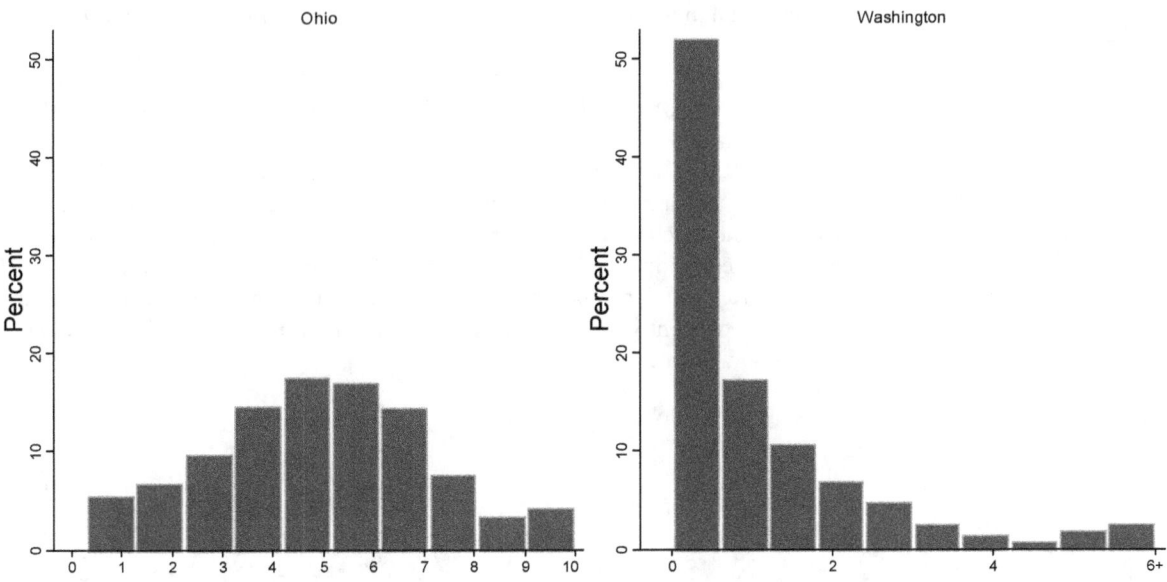

Figure 21. Average Percent Grade

Modeling Methodology

Count data presents two problems to the researcher trying to use standard linear regression techniques: (1) the dependent variable is discrete, taking on only whole number values, and (2) the dependent variable is truncated; that is, no observation can take on a value less than 0. These violations of normality assumptions become even more acute when the data present a very low mean, close to the truncation point.

The Poisson and Negative Binomial GLM Methods

The Poisson distribution can be used to describe count data, though it too requires assumptions about the distribution of the data. Most notably, the Poisson distribution assumes the mean is equal to the variance, both represented by μ. In cases where the data are known to be overdispersed (i.e., the variance is greater than the mean), the NB distribution is often thought to better characterize the data. Moreover, in this situation, the inferences derived from a Poisson regression will systematically mis-represent the significance of the independent variables as the standard errors are incorrect compared to the true values estimated by NB methods.[40] When considered in a regression context, both the Poisson and NB regressions are part of the GLM family, and are estimated via maximum likelihood methods.

The models seek to estimate crashes, μ, as a function of a series of characteristics, x, and the magnitudes of each of the characteristics' effect, β. In this context, μ represents the *weighted average* of the probability that a segment will have a given number of crashes, and thus, implicitly, the predicted number of crashes on that segment. That is:

$$\mu = 0 * P(0 \text{ crashes}) + 1 * P(1 \text{ crash}) + 2 * P(2 \text{ crashes}) + \ldots + n * P(n \text{ crashes}).$$

GLM models are not, however, inherently linear. Thus, a "link function" must be specified to "linearize" the equation so that it resembles ordinary least squares. To clarify, the model equation is shown in [3]. The most common link function, and the one considered "canonical" for the Poisson and NB regression is the log link, which is adopted here. By taking the natural log of both sides, the model appears as in [4] where the dependent variable is in terms of the natural log, and the independent variables are now linear:

$$\mu = e^{\beta_0 + \sum_{j=1}^{k} \beta_j \cdot x_j} \tag{3}$$

$$\ln \mu = \beta_0 + \sum_{j=1}^{k} \beta_j \cdot x_j. \tag{4}$$

The log link also allows for useful interpretations of the estimated coefficients, whereby the coefficient can be considered to be a rough estimate of the *percentage*

---

[40] Land, McCall, and Nagin (1996).

change in the dependant variable with a one-unit increase in the independent variable, when coefficient values are close to zero.[41]

The overdispersion problem is an important one, but is also prone to over-emphasis. To restate, Poisson coefficients are themselves consistent estimators even with over-dispersion but have inaccurate standard errors. The effects of overdispersion have been reduced via the combining of segments to handle the low-exposure problem and by defining a comprehensive model to address issues of heterogeneity. Despite these corrections, the data still appear over-dispersed and so the NB regression model is utilized. The NB model makes more accurate predictions than the Poisson model, without making the severely flawed assumptions of the zero-inflated variations.[42]

Exposure and Crash Rates

The exposure variable methodology allows a few convenient interpretations. First, by using the natural log of the exposure variable, the estimated coefficient can be read as an elasticity. Secondly, it implicitly turns the dependant variable into a rate, illustrated in Equation [5] where the exposure variable is labeled z:

$$
\begin{aligned}
\mu &= e^{\beta_0 + \sum_{j=1}^{k-1} \beta_j \cdot x_j + \beta_k \cdot \ln z} \\
\mu &= e^{\beta_0 + \sum_{j=1}^{k-1} \beta_j \cdot x_j} \, e^{\beta_k \ln z} \\
\mu &= e^{\beta_0 + \sum_{j=1}^{k-1} \beta_j \cdot x_j} \, z^{\beta_k} \qquad [5]\\
\frac{\mu}{z^{\beta_k}} &= e^{\beta_0 + \sum_{j=1}^{k-1} \beta_j \cdot x_j} \\
\ln \frac{\mu}{z^{\beta_k}} &= \beta_0 + \sum_{j=1}^{k-1} \beta_j \cdot x_j
\end{aligned}
$$

In many settings β_k is fixed at 1.0. In this case, however, there is no reason to assume the response of crashes to MVMT is unit elastic, so this model neither fixes the coefficient to 1.0 nor constrains it to a first order variable.

Once applied to HERS, it will be necessary to convert the counts back to crash rates to feed its other modules. This can be simply done after the estimation step.

---

[41] The exact equation for finding the percentage change, regardless of the value, is:

$$\%\Delta\mu = 100 \times (e^{\beta} - 1)$$

[42] Regressions were run using the -poisson- and -nbreg- (negative binomial) commands built into Stata. In all cases, the -robust- option was appended to the commands to utilize robust (also known as White or Sandwich) standard errors. Marginal effects and goodness of fit statistics were computed with the commands in the *Spost* add-on package created by Long and Freese.

Estimating Crash Counts

Comparing Models

In order to capture the complexity of the geometric effects leading to vehicle crashes, several models were estimated and compared. In general, there were first- and second-order models using both Poisson and NB techniques. The model was also simplified to remove a few variables that presented difficulty in establishing a causal connection to crashes.[43] The simplest is a first order model containing each of the variables described above. This is then followed by a model that includes second order effects by way of including squared terms for each of the variables and interactions between the number of curves, intersections, grades, and traffic levels.

As expected, the coefficient values are similar between the Poisson and NB models, seen in Table 12 with the NB model often having lower standard errors. Goodness-of-fit statistics appear in Table 13, and also show generally better fit for the higher order models and for the NB over the Poisson, notably in the AIC and BIC criteria, which are considered two of the more important and easily comparable fit statistics for GLM. The overdispersion factor, alpha, has been further reduced by including the explanatory variables to 0.83, but still fails a likelihood ration test that alpha = 0,[44] further supporting the NB model

An even better idea, however, of how well a model "fits" will come from its predictive ability. Table 14 lists the residuals for 0 to 9 crashes. Both the standard (difference) and Pearson residuals are listed with the smaller residual indicated in *italics*. In the standard residuals, both the Poisson and NB have essentially same total difference (in the "Sum" row) but the NB is more accurate in 9 of the 10 cases. When comparing Pearson residuals (standard residuals weighted and transformed to only positive numbers, thus penalizing a model for being equally "wrong" in opposite directions), the NB also is more accurate in 9 of the 10 cases and far more accurate overall. The standard residual relationship is shown graphically in Figure 22. The squares representing the NB model are consistently closer to the x-axis (where the residual is zero) than the circles representing the Poisson model.

For a final comparison, Figure 23 displays the error in predicting the proportion of segments with 0 to 9 crashes in both the NB and the old, AADT-only model. It is readily apparent that the NB model is more accurate.

---

[43] The initial model includes lanewidth, speed limits, and surface widths. Lane widths are dropped due to the lack of variation in the data and the resulting lack of predictive ability. Speed limits were dropped due to the lack of a plausible causal connection with crashes (see the data description section for details). Surface width was dropped because the various causal relationships are impossible to distinguish given the variety of causes for large surface length (e.g., parking, turning lanes, etc.) and the lack of comparable variables in HPMS for eventual use in HERS. The initial model also included more second-order variables (both squared terms and interactions) but were removed for lack of predictive ability. Information on the process and results from the original runs are in Appendix 1: The Draft 2nd-Order Model

[44] LR test of alpha = 0, chibar2(01) = 31000, p < .001.

Table 12. Comparison of 1st and 2nd Order Poisson and Negative Binomial Regressions

	Poisson (1st)		NegBin (1st)		Poisson		NegBin	
	coef	se	coef	se	coef	se	coef	se
# Curves	0.000	0.010	-0.002	0.009	-0.015	0.017	-0.031	0.019
Avg Curve Length (0.10 miles)	-0.386***	0.038	-0.358***	0.031	-0.365***	0.051	-0.357***	0.047
Avg Curge Degree	0.001	0.001	0.003**	0.001	0.002*	0.001	0.003**	0.001
# Grades	-0.046***	0.005	-0.041***	0.005	-0.097***	0.010	-0.087***	0.010
Avg Grade Length (0.10 miles)	-0.078***	0.015	-0.051***	0.014	-0.114***	0.018	-0.104***	0.015
% Grade	-0.002	0.005	-0.011*	0.006	-0.003	0.006	-0.007	0.007
# Intersections	0.024***	0.003	0.060***	0.003	0.064***	0.005	0.101***	0.005
%age Truck Traffic	-0.016***	0.002	-0.010***	0.002	-0.007	0.004	0.003	0.004
Shoulder Width	-0.091***	0.004	-0.076***	0.003	-0.191***	0.009	-0.181***	0.009
ln(MVMT)	0.808***	0.013	0.700***	0.011	0.818***	0.015	0.852***	0.014
Avg Curve Length (0.10 miles)^2					0.034***	0.011	0.025**	0.010
# Grades^2					0.001**	0.000	0.001**	0.001
Avg Grade Length (0.10 miles)^2					0.001***	0.000	0.001***	0.000
# Intersections^2					-0.001***	0.000	-0.001***	0.000
%age Truck Traffic^2					-0.000**	0.000	-0.001***	0.000
Shoulder Width^2					0.013***	0.001	0.013***	0.001
ln(MVMT)^2					0.073***	0.007	0.074***	0.006
Avg Grade Len * Avg % Grade					0.014***	0.003	0.015***	0.003
# Grades * # Intersections					0.002***	0.001	0.002**	0.001
# Curves * # Grades					0.007***	0.002	0.012***	0.003
ln(MVMT) * # Curves					-0.005	0.010	-0.008	0.010
ln(MVMT) * # Grades					0.010*	0.005	0.003	0.006
ln(MVMT) * # Intersections					-0.016***	0.003	-0.040***	0.003
Constant	1.801***	0.022	1.597***	0.020	1.676***	0.027	1.515***	0.026
ln(alpha)			-0.128***	0.020			-0.188***	0.020

Having chosen the second order NB model, the effects of geometric properties on crashes can be analyzed. The coefficients from above are reproduced in Table 15 along with the Incidence Rate Ratios (IRR), which is the (exact) exponentiated form of the coefficient for determining percent change in the dependent variable.

Estimating the Model and Refinements

Each of the coefficients (or IRRs) reflects a proportionate change in crash counts and cannot be interpreted as a marginal value. Marginal values depend on the existing value of the independent variable for any given segment. For example, ignoring second order and interaction effects, a segment with an average grade length of 0.30 miles and 2.5 predicted crashes would have its predicted number of crashes decrease to 86.6% of the total (2.17 crashes) if the average grade length increased to 0.40 miles. Thus, the marginal effect (0.33 crashes) varies based on the starting value. In reality, the true marginal effect would be the sum of the changes brought about by

Table 13. Goodness of Fit Statistics

	Poisson (1st Degree)	NegBin (1st Degree)	Poisson	NegBin
N	19942	19942	19942	19942
Log-Lik Intercept Only	-107,877.012	-48,926.354	-107,877.012	-48,926.354
Log-Lik Full Model	-59,599.222	-43,033.800	-57,943.056	-42,655.946
Deviation	119,198.445	86,067.600	115,886.111	85,311.892
df(Deviation)	19931	19930	19918	19917
LR	96,555.578	11,785.107	99,867.912	12,540.815
df(LR)	10	10	23	23
Prob > LR	0.000	0.000	0.000	0.000
McFadden's R2	0.448	0.120	0.463	0.128
McFadden's Adj R2	0.447	0.120	0.463	0.128
ML(Cox-Snell) R2	0.992	0.446	0.993	0.467
Cragg-Uhler(Nagelkerke) R2	0.992	0.450	0.993	0.470
AIC	5.978	4.317	5.814	4.281
AIC*n	119,220.445	86,091.600	115,934.111	85,361.892
BIC	-78,130.082	-111,251.026	-81,313.708	-111,878.026
BIC*n	-96,456.573	-11,686.101	-99,640.199	-12,313.101

Table 14. Residuals Based on Predicted Crashes

	Poisson Difference	Poisson Pearson	NegBin Difference	NegBin Pearson
0	0.149	2,466.923	0.023	34.264
1	-0.033	111.273	-0.023	58.213
2	-0.047	289.024	-0.012	25.817
3	-0.034	210.567	-0.005	6.086
4	-0.022	125.232	-0.002	1.902
5	-0.009	28.259	0.004	6.579
6	-0.005	12.371	0.003	5.995
7	-0.004	12.383	0.001	1.060
8	-0.003	5.293	0.001	2.189
9	0.000	0.003	0.003	12.027
Sum	-0.008	3,261.327	-0.008	154.132

Average Grade Length, Average Grade Length squared, and Average Grade Length * Average Grade Degree.

The final column is the exponentiated form representing a *standard deviation change* in the variable (rather than a one-unit change, in the second column). Standard deviations of the independent variables are shown in Table 10 on page 36.

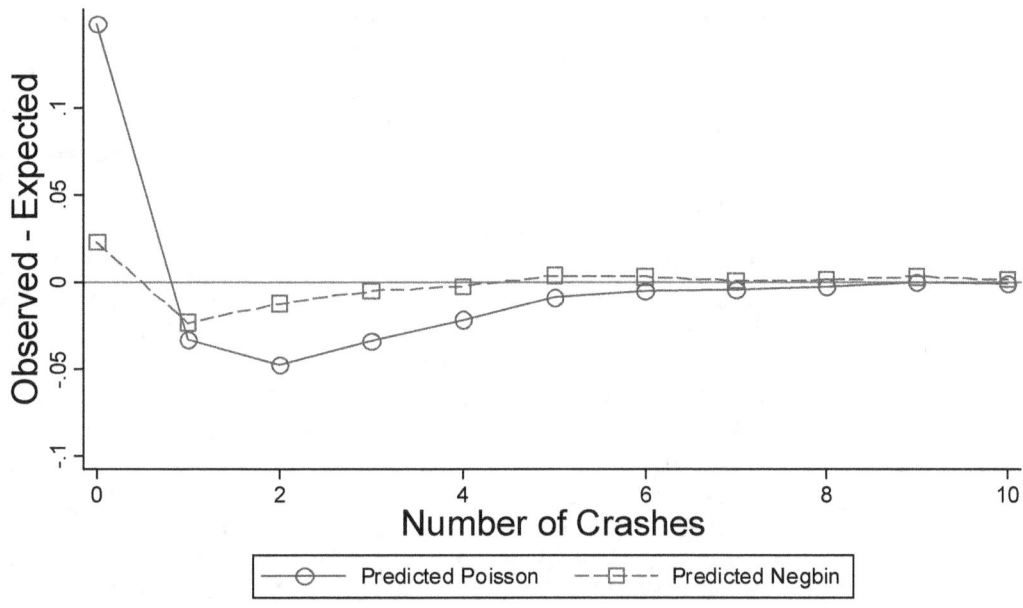

Figure 22. Predicted and Observed Frequencies of Crashes by Poisson and NegBin Models

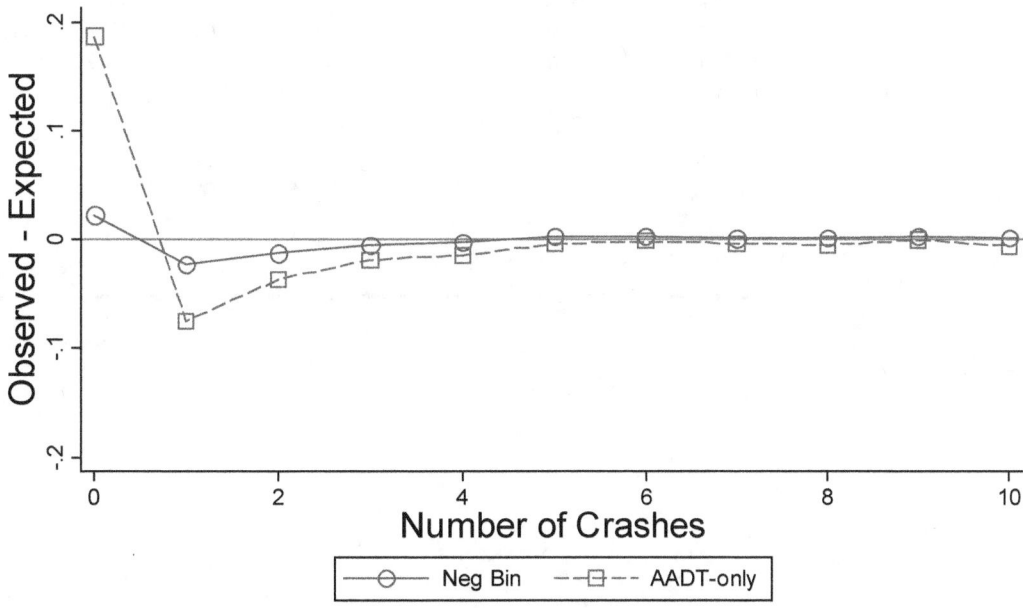

Figure 23. Difference in Observed - Predicted Proportion of Segments by Number of Crashes

Table 15. Coefficients and Incident Rates in the Negative Binomial Regression

	Negative Binomial Regression				
	coef	se		IRR	IRR for a std dev of x
# Curves	-0.031	0.019		0.970	0.972
Avg Curve Length (0.10 miles)	-0.357***	0.047		0.700***	0.882
Avg Curve Length (0.10 miles)^2	0.025**	0.010		1.025**	1.032
Avg Curge Degree	0.003**	0.001		1.003**	1.021
# Grades	-0.087***	0.010		0.916***	0.864
# Grades^2	0.001**	0.001		1.001**	1.033
Avg Grade Length (0.10 miles)	-0.104***	0.015		0.901***	0.866
Avg Grade Length (0.10 miles)^2	0.001***	0.000		1.001***	1.069
% Grade	-0.007	0.007		0.993	0.988
# Intersections	0.101***	0.005		1.107***	1.387
# Intersections^2	-0.001***	0.000		0.999***	0.956
%age Truck Traffic	0.003	0.004		1.003	1.016
%age Truck Traffic^2	-0.001***	0.000		0.999***	0.925
Shoulder Width	-0.181***	0.009		0.834***	0.561
Shoulder Width^2	0.013***	0.001		1.013***	1.459
ln(MVMT)	0.852***	0.014		2.344***	3.064
ln(MVMT)^2	0.074***	0.006		1.077***	1.256
Avg Grade Length * Avg % Grade	0.015***	0.003		1.015***	1.066
# Grades * # Intersections	0.002**	0.001		1.002**	1.025
# Curves * # Grades	0.012***	0.003		1.012***	1.068
ln(MVMT) * # Curves	-0.008	0.010		0.992	0.990
ln(MVMT) * # Grades	0.003	0.006		1.003	1.007
ln(MVMT) * # Intersections	-0.040***	0.003		0.961***	0.797
Constant	1.515***	0.026		4.551***	
ln(alpha)	-0.188***	0.020		0.828***	

significance stars: * 10%, ** 5%, *** 1%

Sensitivity Analysis. Marginal effects in a GLM context are less immediately obvious than in an ordinary least squares model. As the reported coefficients represent percentage changes, the marginal effect depends heavily on the current value of the variable. This complication is compounded with second order effects. To help visualize these changes, Figure 24 shows how crash counts change with changes in explanatory variables. It is important to note that each line assumes that all other variables are held constant at the mean. This remains true even for other variables placed on the same graph. For example, the upper left graph shows that there will be a bit under 3 crashes when there are zero intersections while all other first order variables are held at their respective means. Second order variables are computed based on these first order values.[45] When there are ten intersections, there will be over 6 crashes, assuming that all other first-order variables are held at their means.[46]

Curves. The effect of the number of curves is indeterminate as the standard errors on the estimate are quite high relative to the very small estimated effect. The degree of curvature, while statistically significant has essentially no significance on policy; that is, the actual effect on the number of crashes is imperceptible.[47] While this seems counter-intuitive on the face, it is possible that more attentive or slower driving makes up for the risks posed by more and sharper curves. Curve length, however, is highly significant; longer curves reduce the number of crashes by about 30% for each tenth mile of the curve, though that rate decreases as the length increases.

Grades. Unlike curves, the presence and type of grades appear to have both statistical and policy significance on crashes. Each grade reduces crashes by a bit less than 10% though the rate of decrease itself decreases as seen in the squared term. Much like with curves, this result requires consideration of driver behavior; drivers are likely already using their brakes when on a negative grade and may also slow due to reduced visibility near the top of a positive grade. Additional length to grades exhibits similar effects. The additional length likely gives drivers more time to adapt to the given driving conditions and requires fewer transitions over a given distance. The degree of sharpness to a grade does not have a statistically significant effect on crashes. The interaction term between length and degree is positive and significant, indicating that the combined effect of longer, steeper grades increases the likelihood of a crash more so than merely the effects of each attribute independently, though this combined effect is quite small.

---

[45] In this case, intersections squared is also held at zero. (Curves * Intersections) is computed at the mean number of curves 0.259) times zero intersections, for a total of zero.

[46] In this case, intersections squared is considered to be 100. (Curves * Intersections) is computed at the mean number of curves times 10 intersections, for a total of 2.590.

[47] "Policy significance" is an adaptation of the concept of "economic significance." An example of the latter would be a situation where one can predict with 99% certainty that some variable's affect on a country's GDP is non-zero, but the estimated change is only $3.00.

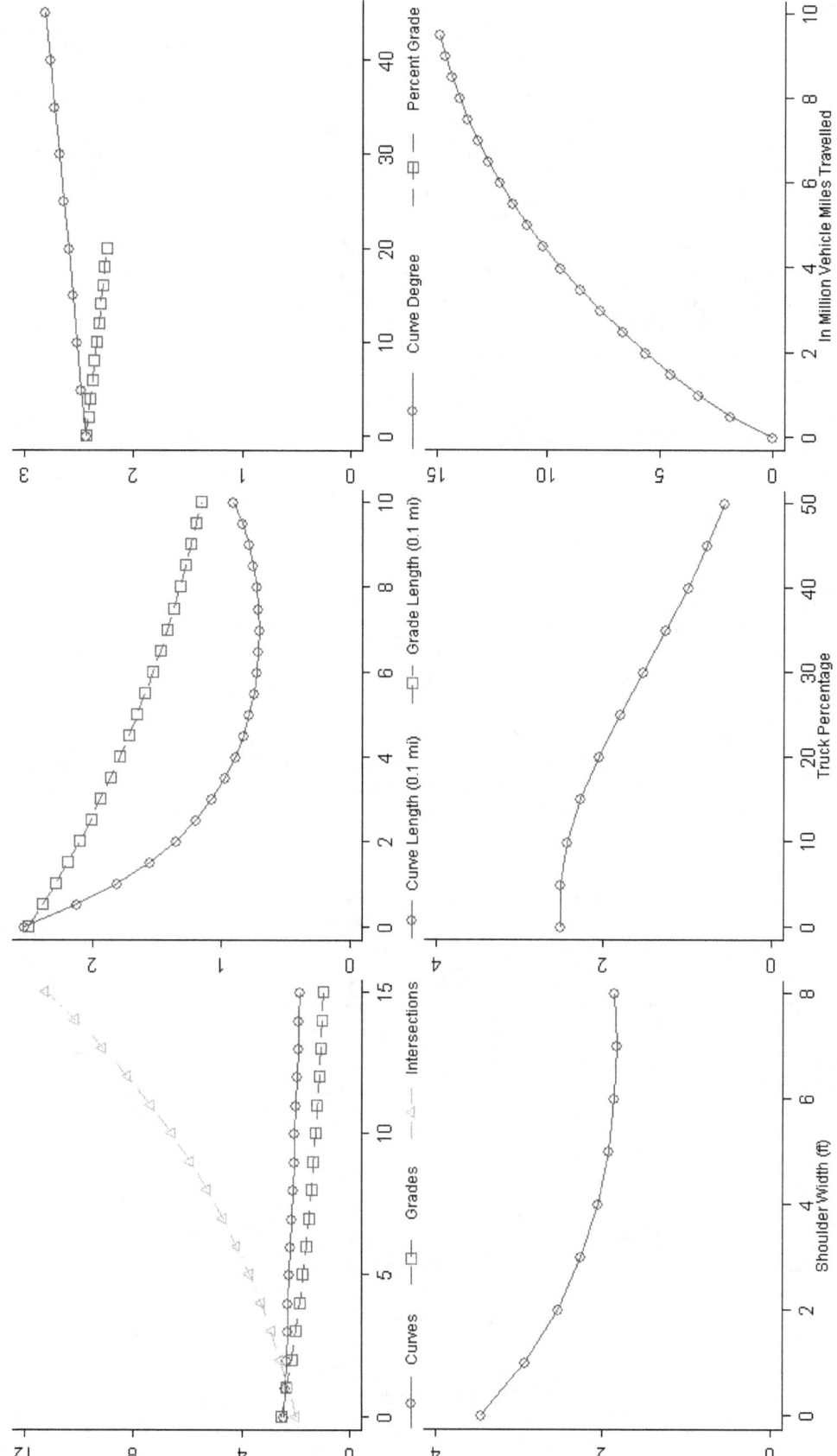

Figure 24. Predicted Crash Rates vs. Values of Explanatory Variables with all Other Variables Held at Mean

Intersections. Unsuprisingly, intersections have a significant and large effect on the number of crashes seen on the roads. Each intersection added increases crashes by about 10%, though the size of the effect decreases slowly as intersections are added.

Percentage of Truck Traffic. Trucks have a significant effect on the number of crashes on road segments. The direction and magnitude of the effect, however, varies considerably based on the current value. Additional truck traffic increase crashes, but at a decreasing rate at low percentages. The second order effect overtakes the first as the percentage of trucks further increases, leading to an overall decrease in crashes. This is likely due to an increase in driver vigilance due to the high proportion of trucks, the lower MVMT on segments with greater truck volume, and that truck drivers are often more skilled and experience fewer crashes.

Shoulder Width. Increased shoulder widths are associated with fewer crashes. Each additional foot decreases crashes by over 16%, though this decrease is itself at a decreasing rate, such that segments with particularly wide shoulders may see an *increase* in crashes. These results are both significant at the 1% level and generally in line with expectations. The squared term's positive value may reflect the increased risk that comes from vehicles entering and leaving the roadway, and that particularly wide shoulders may encourage increased use.

Million Vehicle Miles Traveled. The fact that more vehicles traveling further is associated with significantly more crashes should come as a surprise to no one. This variable and its second order term,[48] however, play an important role in accurately predicting crash counts. Moreover, the use of MVMT rather than AADT, as used in the previous model, allows the current model to account for the occurrence of more crashes on longer segments simply because of the greater length. Despite the triviality of the sign on the coefficient, its value can help researchers understand the relationship between traffic volume and crashes. Because the variable in question is the natural log of MVMT, the coefficient can be interpreted as a pure elasticity. It is then apparent that crash counts are very elastic to changes in traffic levels.

Interactions. Interactions allow the model to include the effect of geometric alignment that is "more than the sum of its parts." The interactions between curves, grades, and intersections are small in magnitude, though both the grades and curves interaction and the grades and intersections interaction are significant at the 5% level. The effect may be small, but in both cases, the combined effect of higher frequencies of the geometric features lead to more crashes, and therefore are an important part of the model. The interaction between MVMT and grades is insignificant, though positive. The combination of curves and increased traffic leads to an insignificant decrease in crashes while the interaction between traffic and intersections is negative and highly significant. This latter effect is potentially due to the reduced possibility for crashes when there is less movement on the road in the first place.

---

[48] Note that the second order term is the square of the natural log of MVMT, not the natural log of MVMT squared.

Accuracy in Washington and Ohio

As a quick and simple robustness check, the model was re-run for both Washington and Ohio individually. While it does not guarantee the model will be perfectly applicable to other states, it at least helps narrow down the possibility that model accuracy is due to a particular state-specific effect that overwhelms the other state's data. Figure 25 contains the predicted residuals in proportion of segments with between 0 and 9 crashes. When comparing to Figure 23, be sure to note the different scale on the vertical axis. The model is seen to be quite accurate for both states, though, particularly at low crash counts, the accuracy is a bit better in Ohio than Washington. This is likely due to the larger quantity of road segment data obtained from Ohio.

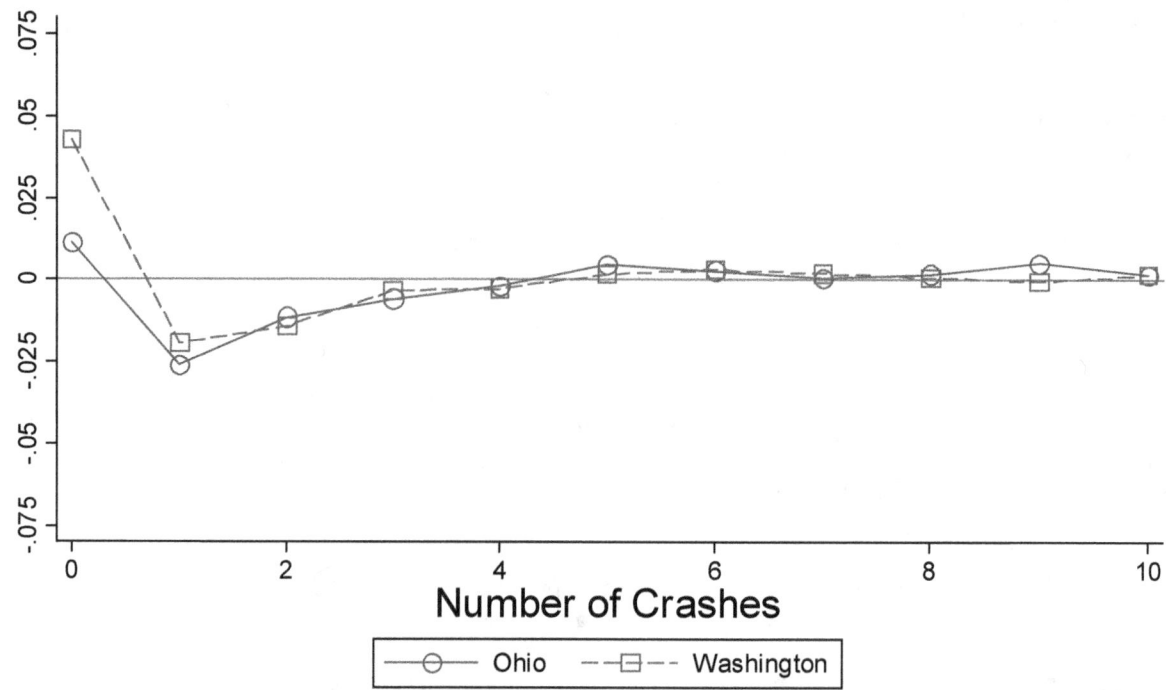

Figure 25. Difference in Observed - Predicted Proportion of Crashes in Ohio and Washington

Translating Between HSIS and HPMS Variables

The data used to generate the estimates in the previous section came from the FHWA HSIS database. However, the HERS model is populated with information from HPMS.[49] The basic road information contained in each database is broadly similar but the coding details for each field can vary between the two. This section describes how to turn HPMS data into the variables used in generating this model.

Truck Percentage, Lane Width. Truck percentage and lane widths are fields that exist in HPMS that do not require any translation to include in the model.

Intersections. HPMS contains three entries relating to intersections: those with signals, stop signs, and other. To prepare data for the crash model, simply sum these three variables.

Shoulder Width. HPMS keeps separate fields for shoulder widths on each side of the street. As not all states maintain this level of detail in HSIS, it is necessary to average the two values for use in the model. That is, the input should be as shown in Equation [6].

$$\text{Shoulder Width} = \frac{\text{Left Shoulder Width} + \text{Right Shoulder Width}}{2} \qquad [6]$$

MVMT. MVMT is not in HPMS but is easily calculated from existing information. The formula is noted above in Equation [2] on page 38.

Curves and Grades. HPMS considers curves and grades in classes rather than recording exact degrees of curvature as is done with HSIS data. A compromise, then, must be found between the HPMS classifications and the more detailed analysis possible with HSIS data. The next sections discuss HPMS and newly created variables, comparisons to the original model variables, and the development of a modified crash model using these new variables.

New Variables and Comparisons

The model used so far includes three variables relating to grades or curves. They count the number present, the average percent grade or curve degree, and the average length of the grades or curves over the segment. As HPMS only provides aggregate information by grade or degree class, the exact number of grades or degrees, as well as any average values, are unknown. Three new variables are used instead: 1) the number of grade or curve classes present on a segment, 2) the total length of all grades or curves over the segment, and 3) a weighted value of the percent grade or degree of curvature. Comparative summary statistics appear in Table 16.

---

[49] HSIS data were used for the development of the model because HPMS does not contain crash information.

Table 16. Summary Statistics for Newly Created Variables to Apply to HPMS Data and the HSIS Variables they are Replacing

	mean	sd	min	p25	p50	p75	max
# Curves	0.259	0.930	0.000	0.000	0.000	0.000	28.000
# Curve Classes	0.199	0.530	0.000	0.000	0.000	0.000	5.000
# Grades	0.597	1.676	0.000	0.000	0.000	1.000	31.000
# Grade Classes	0.363	0.704	0.000	0.000	0.000	1.000	5.000
Avg Curve Length in 1/10th miles	0.094	0.351	0.000	0.000	0.000	0.000	9.100
Total Curve Length (miles)	0.021	0.072	0.000	0.000	0.000	0.000	1.200
Avg Grade Length in 1/10th miles	0.331	1.382	0.000	0.000	0.000	0.100	66.300
Total Grade Length (miles)	0.081	0.282	0.000	0.000	0.000	0.020	7.510
Avg Curve Degree	1.539	7.478	0.000	0.000	0.000	0.000	96.000
Weighted Curve Degree	1.907	8.240	0.000	0.000	0.000	0.000	96.000
Avg Grade Percent	0.591	1.630	0.000	0.000	0.000	0.005	18.000
Weighted Percent Grade	0.517	1.706	0.000	0.000	0.000	0.000	18.000

Class Counts. The grade or curve class count should broadly resemble, but is constrained to being less than or equal to, the total number of grades or curves. That is, only one grade or curve of each class type will be counted in the new variable whereas multiples could exist before. While the bias introduced here could theoretically be large, the evidence from Ohio and Washington imply it will be minimal. For example, 85% of segments contain no curves, while another 12% contain only 1 curve. Thus, it is assured that the number of curve classes will equal the number of total curves in at least 97% of all observations. Similarly, 74% of segments contain no grades and 14% of segments contain only one, resulting in at least an 88% match between the two. The relationship between curve or grade counts and crashes is similar to the relationship between crashes and the number of grade or curve classes. This can be seen in Figure 26 and Figure 27. Recall that 90% of segments appear in the leftmost two boxes for each graph, causing the greater variation in box appearance for larger counts. Moreover, as Ohio's HSIS sample contained no very small grades, it is impossible for there to be any segments with all 5 grade classes.

Total Lengths. HPMS contains information on the total length of the grades or curves that make up each class. This variable is merely the sum of the length associated with each grade or curve class. Total length has the advantage of not being dependent on the number of curves or grades in the segment, as the number is not available in HPMS. Histograms of average and total grade and curve length (by state) can been seen in Figure 28 and Figure 29. Note these graphs are only for segments which have at least one grade or curve. 74% of segments have a total grade length of 0 and 85% of segments have a total curve length of 0 as well.

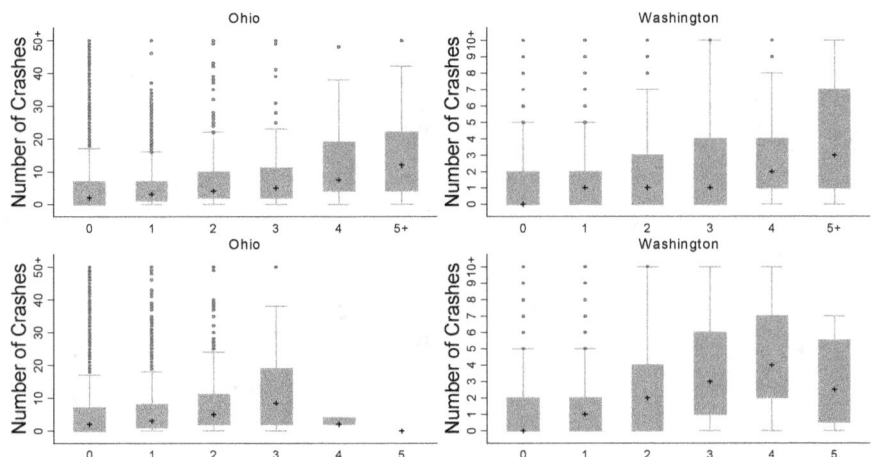

Figure 26. Crash Count by Number of Grades (above) and Number of Grade Classes (below)

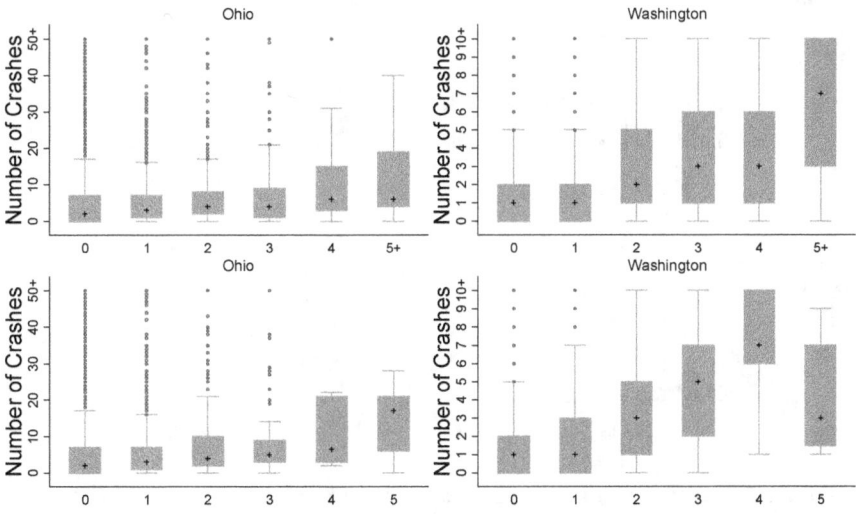

Figure 27. Crash Count by Number of Curves (above) and Number of Curve Classes (below)

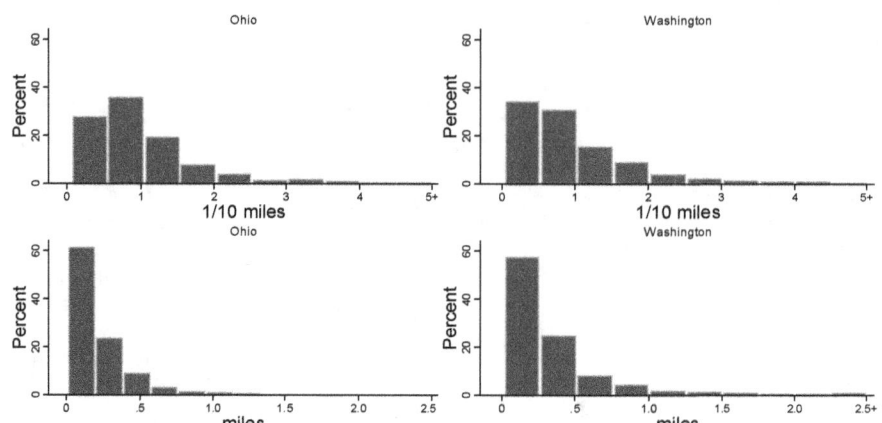

Figure 28. Average Grade Length (above) and Total Grade Length (below)

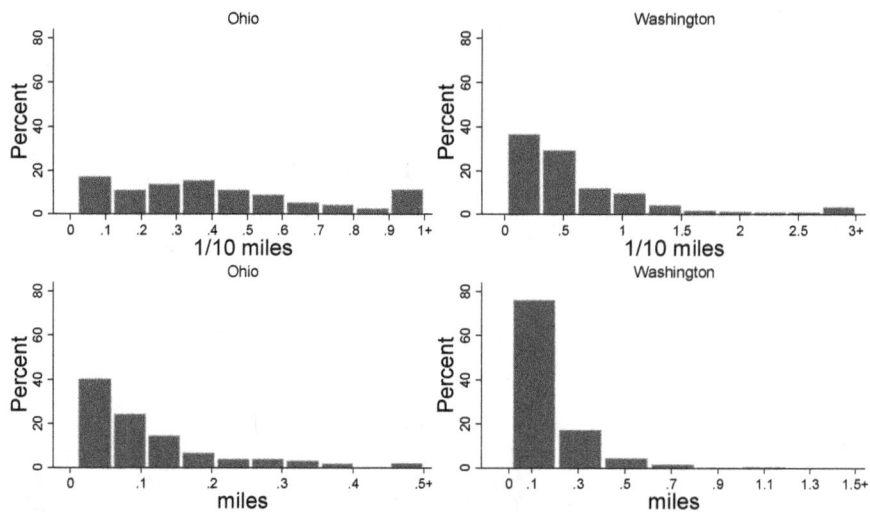

Figure 29. Average Curve Length (above) and Total Curve Length (below)

Weighted Percent/Degree. This variable is constructed from the HPMS fields on the grade/curve classes present and their total length. The formulas to create these variables from the original HSIS data are shown in Equations [7] and [8].

$$\text{Segment Weighted Percent Grade HSIS} = \begin{cases} 0 & , \# \text{ Grades} = 0 \\ \dfrac{\sum\limits_{i=1}^{\# \text{ Grades}} (\text{Grade Length}_i \cdot \text{Percent Grade}_i)}{\sum\limits_{i=1}^{\# \text{ Grades}} \text{Grade Length}_i} & , \# \text{ Grades} \geq 1 \end{cases} \quad [7]$$

$$\text{Segment Weighted Curve Degree HSIS} = \begin{cases} 0 & , \# \text{ Curves} = 0 \\ \dfrac{\sum\limits_{i=1}^{\# \text{ Curves}} (\text{Curve Length}_i \cdot \text{Curve Degree}_i)}{\sum\limits_{i=1}^{\# \text{ Curves}} \text{Curve Length}_i} & , \# \text{ Curves} \geq 1 \end{cases} \quad [8]$$

Though not a measure of average degree, it shares characteristics with average degree as it is a score that is based on the magnitude of the grade or curve controlled for the total length of grades or curves on the segment. Figure 30 and Figure 31 are histograms of the average percent grade and degree, as well as the weighted percent grade and degree. While the histograms broadly track one another, it is important to remember that grades under 3% are not reported in Ohio's HSIS sample leading to the "missing" left side on the graph.

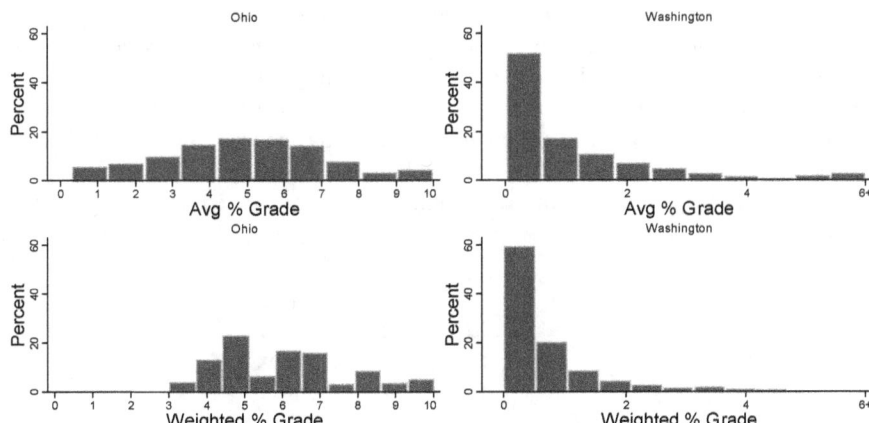

Figure 30. Average Percent Grade (above) and Weighted Percent Grade (below)

Because this measure is not dependent on the total number of grades or curves present on a segment, these variables do not risk exacerbating any bias of using the curve and grade class counts.

These variables can be computed with HPMS data solely from the information on the total length of grades or curves by class and a lookup table of equating each grade or curve class to a particular percent grade or curvature degree. To arrive at this particu-

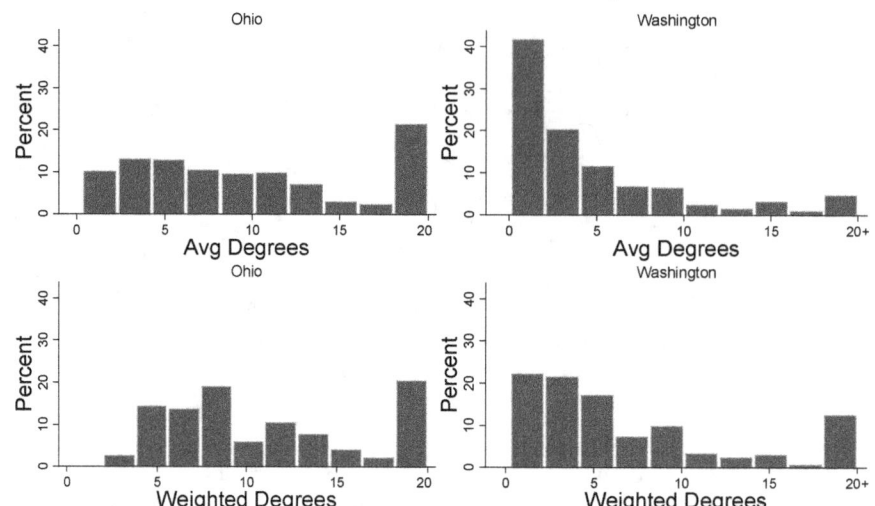

Figure 31. Average Curve Degree (above) and Weighted Curve Degree (below)

lar crosswalk, a multi-step process was undertaken. First, a kernel density plot was generated. This plot represents an estimated probability distribution function based on the actual observed data, and can be interpreted like a smoothed histogram. The next step was to identify the points where the density plot intersects the changes in grade or degree class and to connect them linearly. For Class F, the slope over the area near the division was extrapolated down to the y-axis, cutting off the long tail extending to the right. As an example, the plot for percent grade can be seen in Figure 32. To find the appropriate percent grade/degree value to apply to each class, the x-coordinate for the center of mass for each class type was calculated using equation [9] where m and b represent the slope between the two points and the computed y-intercept, respectively.

$$Center_x = \frac{\int x \cdot f(x)dx}{\int f(x)dx} = \frac{\int x(mx + b)dx}{\int (mx + b)dx} \qquad [9]$$

See Table 17 and Table 18 for the percent grade and curve degree to assign, respectively, by class. The equations to calculate the weighted percent grade and curve degree from HPMS are shown in Equations [10] and [11].

$$\text{Segment Weighted} \atop \text{Percent Grade HPMS} = \frac{\sum_{i=A}^{F} (\text{Grade Length}_i \cdot \text{Assigned Percent Grade}_i)}{\sum_{i=A}^{F} \text{GradeLength}_i} \qquad [10]$$

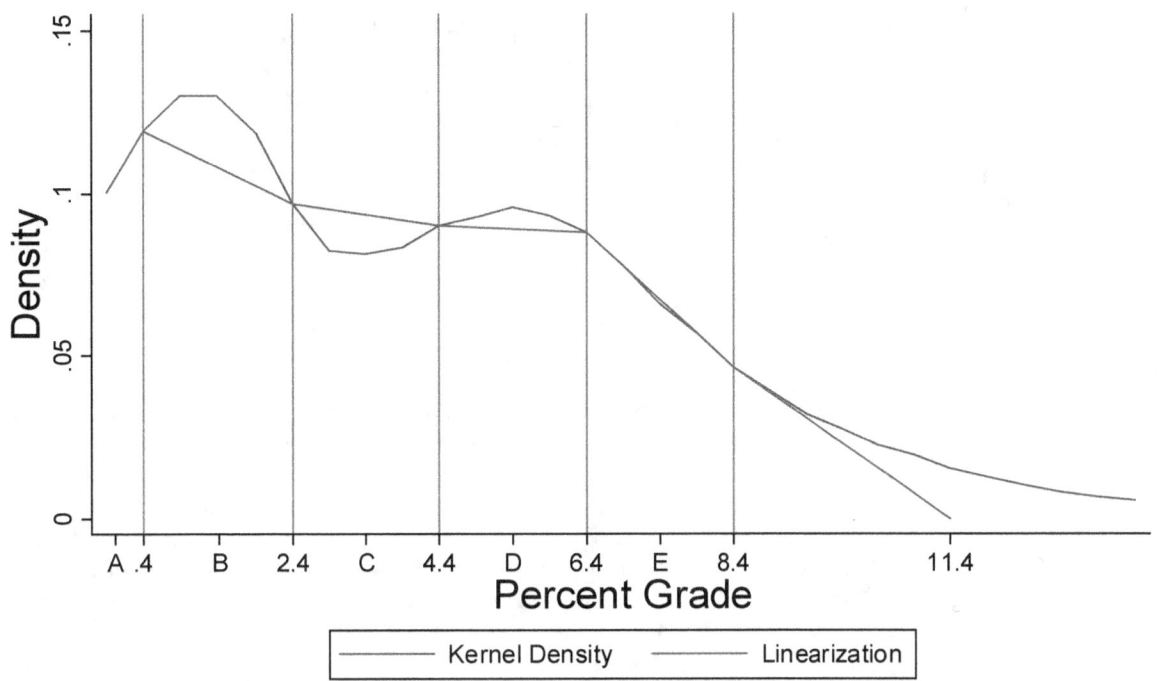

Figure 32. Density Plot Used for Grade Class Conversions

Table 17. Assigned Percent Grades for HPMS Grade Classes

Grade Class	Percent Grades in Class	Assigned Percent Grade
A	0.0-0.4	0.2
B	0.5-2.4	1.4
C	2.5-4.4	3.4
D	4.5-6.4	5.4
E	6.5-8.4	7.3
F	8.5+	9.4

$$\text{Segment Weighted Curve Degree HPMS} = \frac{\sum_{i=A}^{F} (\text{Curve Length}_i \cdot \text{Assigned Curve Degree}_i)}{\sum_{i=A}^{F} \text{Curve Length}_i} \qquad [11]$$

Table 18. Assigned Curve Degrees for HPMS Curve Classes

Curve Class	Curve Degrees in Class	Assigned Curve Degree
A	00.0-03.4	2.0
B	03.5-05.4	4.4
C	05.5-08.4	6.9
D	08.5-13.9	10.9
E	14.0-27.9	19.3
F	28+	29.0

The Revised Regression

Using the variables generated as above, the regression was re-run to check for consistency in results; the results are displayed in Table 19. For variables that did not change between the two models, the coefficients and significance levels are virtually identical. The sign on the coefficient for all previously significant variables remains the same and only in one case (grade classes squared) does a previously significant variable fail to again pass that threshold. Variables relating to the number of curve classes (including interactions) and weighted percent grade now are statistically significant at conventional levels.

This can be seen graphically in Figure 33, which replicates the sensitivity analysis in Figure 24 on page 56. The shapes of the curves are highly similar to the original model. The upper limit on grade and class counts truncates the lines earlier, and the magnitude of the dip in curve length graph has been reduced, but both graphs retain the same general shape as in the HSIS model. The predicted proportion of segments experiencing particular crash counts varies nearly imperceptibly between the two models, as seen in Figure 34.

These results confirm that the application of the new variables to translate between HSIS and HPMS data do a sufficient job of maintaining the crash model developed above while also being practicable within HERS.

HERS has been designed to output crash results in terms of the crash rate per AADT. The final step is to convert the predicted crash count returned by the model into this rate by dividing the crash count by AADT, shown in Equation [12].

$$\text{Crash Rate} = \frac{\text{Crash Count}}{\text{AADT}} \qquad [12]$$

In the following section, the final (HPMS) model is summarized for inclusion within HERS.

Table 19. Comparison of Negative Binomial Regressions on HPMS and HSIS Variables

Negative Binomial Regression				
	HPMS		HSIS	
	coef	se	coef	se
# Curve Classes	-0.142***	0.034		
# Curves			-0.030	0.019
Total Curve Length	-1.206***	0.307		
Total Curve Length^2	0.747*	0.439		
Avg Curve Length (0.10 miles)			-0.365***	0.048
Avg Curve Length (0.10 miles)^2			0.026***	0.010
Weighted Curve Degree	0.003**	0.001		
Avg Curve Degree			0.003**	0.001
# Grade Classes	-0.151***	0.057		
# Grade Classes^2	0.006	0.017		
# Grades			-0.087***	0.009
# Grades^2			0.001**	0.001
Total Grade Length	-0.497***	0.102		
Total Grade Length^2	0.071***	0.016		
Avg Grade Length (0.10 miles)			-0.097***	0.016
Avg Grade Length (0.10 miles)^2			0.001***	0.000
Weighted Grade Percent	-0.022**	0.009		
Avg Grade Percent			-0.009	0.007
# Intersections	0.100***	0.005	0.102***	0.005
# Intersections^2	-0.001**	0.000	-0.001***	0.000
%age Truck Traffic	0.003	0.004	0.003	0.004
%age Truck Traffic^2	-0.001***	0.000	-0.001***	0.000
Shoulder Width	-0.177***	0.009	-0.181***	0.009
Shoulder Width^2	0.013***	0.001	0.013***	0.001
ln(MVMT)	0.869***	0.015	0.852***	0.014
ln(MVMT)^2	0.077***	0.006	0.074***	0.006
Total Grade Length * Weighted Percent Grade	0.111***	0.020		
Avg Grade Length * Avg Percent Grade			0.015***	0.003
# Grade Classes * # Intersections	0.010***	0.003		
# Grades * # Intersections			0.002**	0.001
# Curve Classes * # Grade Classes	0.072***	0.014		
# Curves * # Grades			0.012***	0.003
ln(MVMT) * # Curve Classes	0.034**	0.016		
ln(MVMT) * # Curves			-0.008	0.010
ln(MVMT) * # Grade Classes	-0.030**	0.015		
ln(MVMT) * # Grades			0.003	0.006
ln(MVMT) * # Intersections	-0.042***	0.003	-0.040***	0.003
Constant	1.521***	0.026	1.515***	0.026
/lnalpha	-0.189***	0.020	-0.188***	0.020
significance stars: * 10%, ** 5%, *** 1%				

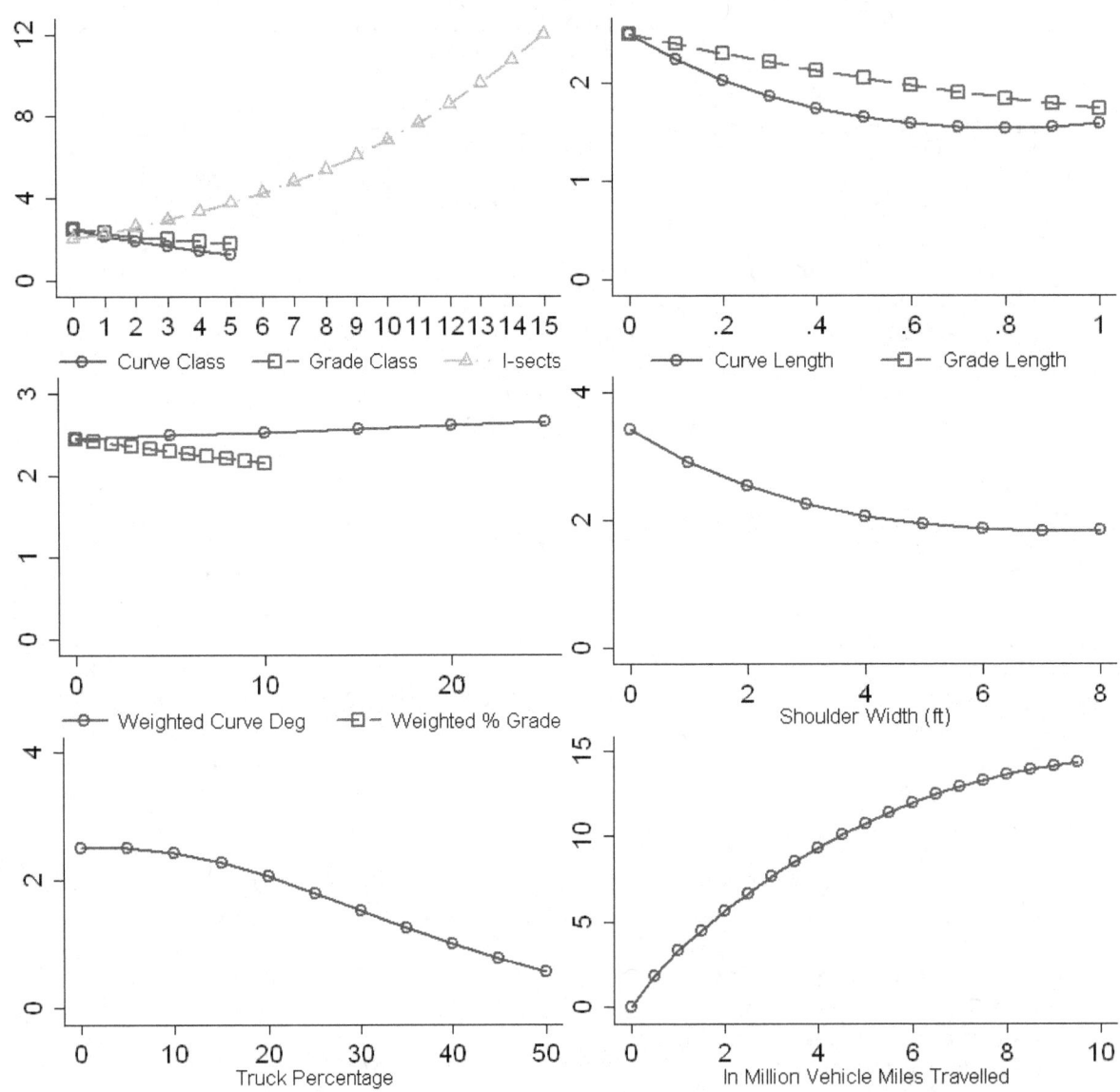

Figure 33. Predicted Crash Rates vs. Values of Explanatory Variables with all Other Variables Held at Mean for HPMS model

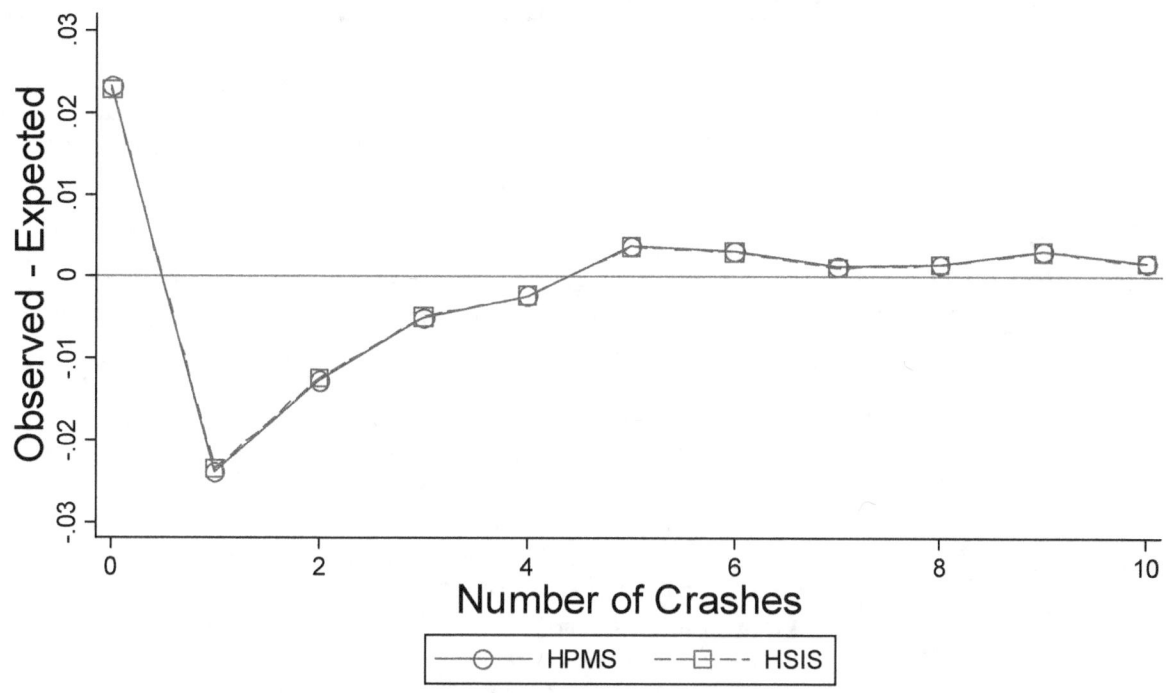

Figure 34. Difference in Observed - Predicted Proportion of Segments by Number of Crashes for HPMS and HSIS models

The Implemented Crash Model

This section contains all of the necessary information to implement the new, two-lane urban crash model within HERS. The model is composed of a crash prediction equation (expressed as a rate) and formulas to generate the independent variables not already in HPMS.

The Crash Prediction Equation

$$
\begin{aligned}
\text{Crash Rate} = (\,&1.52083 - 0.14158\,\text{Curve Class Count} \\
&- 1.20624\,\text{Total Curve Length} - 0.74739\,\text{TotalCurveLength}^2 \\
&+ 0.00339\,\text{Weighted Curve Degree} - 0.15068\,\text{Grade Class Count} \\
&+ 0.00584\,\text{Grade Class Count}^2 - 0.49689\,\text{Total Grade Length} \\
&+ 0.07123\,\text{Total Grade Length}^2 - 0.02238\,\text{Weighted Grade Percent} \\
&+ 0.10050\,\text{Intersection Count} - 0.00072\,\text{Intersection Count}^2 \\
&+ 0.00333\,\text{Truck Percentage} - 0.00066\,\text{Truck Percentage}^2 \\
&- 0.17693\,\text{Shoulder Width} + 0.01252\,\text{Shoulder Width}^2 \\
&+ 0.86854\ln(\text{MVMT}) + 0.07741(\ln(\text{MVMT}))^2 \\
&+ 0.11092(\text{Total Grade Length} \cdot \text{Weighted Grade Percent}) \\
&+ 0.00998(\text{Grade Class Count} \cdot \text{Intersection Count}) \\
&+ 0.07244(\text{Curve Class Count} \cdot \text{Grade Class Count}) \\
&+ 0.03361(\ln(\text{MVMT}) \cdot \text{Curve Class Count}) \\
&- 0.02976(\ln(\text{MVMT}) \cdot \text{Grade Class Count}) \\
&- 0.04234(\ln(\text{MVMT}) \cdot \text{Intersection Count}))\,/\,\text{AADT}
\end{aligned}
$$

[13]

Formulas for Independent Variables

$$
\begin{aligned}
\text{Curve Class Count} =\ & \begin{cases} 0, & \text{Length of Curve Class A} = 0 \\ 1, & \text{Length of Curve Class A} > 0 \end{cases} + \begin{cases} 0, & \text{Length of Curve Class B} = 0 \\ 1, & \text{Length of Curve Class B} > 0 \end{cases} \\
& + \begin{cases} 0, & \text{Length of Curve Class C} = 0 \\ 1, & \text{Length of Curve Class C} > 0 \end{cases} + \begin{cases} 0, & \text{Length of Curve Class D} = 0 \\ 1, & \text{Length of Curve Class D} > 0 \end{cases} \\
& + \begin{cases} 0, & \text{Length of Curve Class E} = 0 \\ 1, & \text{Length of Curve Class E} > 0 \end{cases} + \begin{cases} 0, & \text{Length of Curve Class F} = 0 \\ 1, & \text{Length of Curve Class F} > 0 \end{cases}
\end{aligned}
$$

[14]

$$
\begin{aligned}
\text{Total Curve Length} =\ & \text{Length of Curve Class A} + \text{Length of Curve Class B} \\
& + \text{Length of Curve Class C} + \text{Length of Curve Class D} \\
& + \text{Length of Curve Class E} + \text{Length of Curve Class F}
\end{aligned}
$$

[15]

$$
\text{Weighted Curve Degree} = \frac{\left(\begin{array}{l} \text{Length of Curve Class A} \cdot 2.0 + \text{Length of Curve Class B} \cdot 4.4 \\ + \text{Length of Curve Class C} \cdot 6.9 + \text{Length of Curve Class D} \cdot 10.9 \\ + \text{Length of Curve Class E} \cdot 19.3 + \text{Length of Curve Class F} \cdot 29.0 \end{array}\right)}{\left(\begin{array}{l} \text{Length of Curve Class A} + \text{Length of Curve Class B} \\ + \text{Length of Curve Class C} + \text{Length of Curve Class D} \\ + \text{Length of Curve Class E} + \text{Length of Curve Class F} \end{array}\right)}
$$

[16]

$$\text{Grade Class Count} = \begin{cases} 0, & \text{Length of Grade Class A} = 0 \\ 1, & \text{Length of Grade Class A} > 0 \end{cases} + \begin{cases} 0, & \text{Length of Grade Class B} = 0 \\ 1, & \text{Length of Grade Class B} > 0 \end{cases}$$

$$+ \begin{cases} 0, & \text{Length of Grade Class C} = 0 \\ 1, & \text{Length of Grade Class C} > 0 \end{cases} + \begin{cases} 0, & \text{Length of Grade Class D} = 0 \\ 1, & \text{Length of Grade Class D} > 0 \end{cases}$$

$$+ \begin{cases} 0, & \text{Length of Grade Class E} = 0 \\ 1, & \text{Length of Grade Class E} > 0 \end{cases} + \begin{cases} 0, & \text{Length of Grade Class F} = 0 \\ 1, & \text{Length of Grade Class F} > 0 \end{cases} \quad [17]$$

$$\text{Total Grade Length} = \begin{array}{l} \text{Length of Grade Class A} + \text{Length of Grade Class B} \\ + \text{Length of Grade Class C} + \text{Length of Grade Class D} \\ + \text{Length of Grade Class E} + \text{Length of Grade Class F} \end{array} \quad [18]$$

$$\text{Weighted Grade Percent} = \frac{\left(\begin{array}{l} \text{Length of Grade Class A} \cdot 0.2 + \text{Length of Grade Class B} \cdot 1.4 \\ + \text{Length of Grade Class C} \cdot 3.4 + \text{Length of Grade Class D} \cdot 5.4 \\ + \text{Length of Grade Class E} \cdot 7.3 + \text{Length of Grade Class F} \cdot 9.4 \end{array}\right)}{\left(\begin{array}{l} \text{Length of Grade Class A} + \text{Length of Grade Class B} \\ + \text{Length of Grade Class C} + \text{Length of Grade Class D} \\ + \text{Length of Grade Class E} + \text{Length of Grade Class F} \end{array}\right)} \quad [19]$$

$$\text{Intersection Count} = \begin{array}{l} \text{Number of Signal Intersections} + \text{Number of Stop Sign Intersections} \\ + \text{Number of Other Intersections} \end{array} \quad [20]$$

$$\text{Shoulder Width} = \frac{\text{Left Shoulder Width} + \text{Right Shoulder Width}}{2} \quad [21]$$

$$\text{MVMT} = \frac{\text{AADT} \times 365 \times \text{Segment Length}}{1,000,000} \quad [22]$$

Further Research

Adjustments to the HERS crash model fit into three broad categories: expanding across functional classes, incorporating data from additional states to refine coefficients, and in the longer term, utilizing more advanced modeling techniques. Notably in this latter category would be attempts to include predictions of crash severity in the model as well as the use of multi-year data that can take into account the history of a particular segment.

In all of these cases, there must be further improvements in data development. Even within HSIS data, there are sometimes wide swaths of data unavailable or unreliable, reducing the potential sample.[50] As data recording has improved, standards and definitions in the data have changed, making year-to-year comparisons difficult. While these developments are welcome, stability in data gathering techniques as well as in section endpoints will allow for richer uses of the data.

Facility Types. This exercise has been limited to urban two-lane roads but the methodology can be utilized across other facility types. While none of the other facility types have a current model in as much need of upgrade as two-lane urban streets, nearly all of the other facility type models do not utilize all of the available and applicable inventory elements contained within HMPS. Moreover, as mentioned earlier, changes to the roadway that cause the segment to change facility types may lead to a implausibly large change in predicted crashes. Models that smooth the edges in predictions across facility types should be investigated.

Additional States. The model detailed above utilizes HSIS data gathered from Ohio and Washington. Although HSIS remains the only way to systematically combine crash and geometric information, there are more participating HSIS states. Washington and Ohio presented the best collection of attributes and crash information of the HSIS states on which to base estimates but the addition of other states can help to refine the coefficients and improve accuracy.

Severity Models. Currently, crash severity is predicted by using national averages of severity classes to create a multiplier used against the predicted crash total. The methodology has some significant flaws in that it cannot take into account even state-specific factors that may affect the severity distribution much less roadway- or segment-specific factors. Critically, it also does not allow geometric changes to affect a change in the distribution of crashes. Two categories of severity models should be investigated, simultaneous models and two-stage models.

Simultaneous or multi-level models estimate multiple models concurrently to predict the number of crashes causing each level of injury (fatality, injury, property damage only). These models may, but do not necessarily, contain the same set of variables, and attention should be paid to determining the right variables necessary to differenti-

---

[50] For example, a large portion of urban crashes in Ohio were not included in the data set until 2002, making data from before this time unusable.

ate severity levels. This technique could be of great value to the HERS modeling process but the use of simultaneous methods for count models is quite new, and given the significant upgrade achieved with the current methods, it is prudent to let this method develop further before applying it here.

Another option is a multi-stage model where the results of the crash prediction model are fed into a series of follow-up models that predict the proportion of crashes of each severity level. In these multi-stage models, additional variables that affect crash severity are added. The Federal Rail Administration utilizes a model of this type for grade crossings where the proportion of fatal and casualty accidents are estimated and then injury and property damage only accidents are computed as a function of the estimates.[51] It should be noted that these two techniques are not mutually exclusive as one could use simultaneous methods to predict crash severity but a single model to predict the total crash count.

Panel Models. Panel data gathered over multiple years would allow the model to better separate the random variation in crashes from those due to segment-specific geometry. Additionally, a panel model can take into account changes over time in overall driving or safety patterns. A branch of models within this area, called Empirical Bayes (EB), are of particular interest. EB models directly incorporate a previous year's crash count into the prediction of the current year, further improving the performance of the model when it is believed there are idiosyncrasies innate to segments.

Any panel method would require more years of HSIS data gathered using techniques that do not vary significantly from year to year, as well as stability in the identification of segments from year to year. Neither of those requirements look likely to be met in the near time, but it remains a possibility to investigate after the revision of models for other functional classes.

It is recommended that further research take place in the order presented in this section. The revision of additional functional classes will provide immediate benefits to the HERS model while the addition of more states to modelling process will help make medium-term adjustments to the model, allowing it to be fine-tuned, rather than entirely reworked as in the current document. Smoothing the edges between the various facility type models will help ensure that *any* geometric change (rather than changes that keep a segment within a facility type) will lead to a reasonable change in predicted crashes.

The adoption of even more advanced modelling techniques could potentially improve model results but would require improvements in data collection. In all cases, revisions to the method of applying costs to crashes also warrants attention, particularly in light of recent guidance from the Secretary of Transportation adjusting the cost of a

---

[51] Lee, Douglass B., *et al.*, John A. Volpe National Transportation Systems Center, Department of Transportation, *Benefit-Cost Evaluation of a Highway-Railroad Intermodal Control System (ICS)*, prepared for: Alstom, New York State Department of Transportation, Federal Highway Administration, *et al.*, (June, 2004).

human life. Regardless, there remains much work to be done in the development of HERS crash modelling.

6. References

Bowman, B L, and R L Vecellio, "Effect of Urban and Suburban Median Types on Both Vehicular and Pedestrian Safety," *Transportation Research Record*, Transportation Research Board:1445 (1994), pp. 169-179.

Camus, Gregorio, and Herbert Weinblatt, Volpe National Transportation Systems Center, U.S. Department of Transportation, *Highway Economic Requirements System: Technical Report*, Vol. IV, prepared for: Federal Highway Administration, (December, 2000).

Cirillo, J.A., *Access Control*, Vol. I of VI, *Safety Effectiveness of Highway Design Features*, prepared for: Federal Highway Administration (1992).

Designing Safer Roads: Practices for Resurfacing, Restoration, and Rehabilitation, prepared for: Transportation Research Board, Washington, D.C., National Research Council, Special Report 214 (1987).

"Fatality Analysis Reporting System," Available at: http://www-nrd nhtsa.dot.gov/pdf/nrd-30/NCSA/FARS/809-726/index htm (Last Accessed: November 24, 2004).

Harwood, Douglas W., *et al.*, Federal Highway Administration, U.S. Department of Transportation, *Development of SPFs for Safety Analyst: Interim Tools*, (October, 2004).

Highway Infrastructure: FHWA's Model for Estimating Highway Needs Is Generally Reasonable, Despite Limitations, General Accounting Office, (June, 2000).

Highway Performance Monitoring System: Field Manual, Federal Highway Administration, U.S. Department of Transportation, (2000).

"Highway Safety Information System," Available at: www hsis.org (Last Accessed: November 18, 2004).

Highway Safety: Research Continues on a Variety of Factors That Contribute to Motor Vehicle Crashes, Government Accounting Office, (March, 2003).

Highway Statistics, Federal Highway Administration, U.S. Department of Transportation, (2003).

Hughes, Warren, *et al.*, "Development of a Highway Safety Manual," *NCHRP Web Document*, 62 (March, 2004).

"Interactive Highway Safety Design Model," Available at: http://www.tfhrc.gov/safety/ihsdm/ (Last Accessed: November 18, 2004).

Kuciemba, S. R., and J. A. Cirillo, Federal Highway Administration, U.S. Department of Transportation, *Intersections*, Vol. V of VI, *Safety Effectiveness of Highway Design Features*, FHWA/RD-91/048 (1992).

Land, Kenneth C., *et al.*, "A Comparison of Poisson, Negative Binomial, and Semi-parametric Mixed Poisson Regression Models with Empirical Applications to Criminal Careers Data," *Sociological Methods & Research*, 24:4 (May, 1996), pp. 387-442.

Lee, Douglass B., *et al.*, Volpe National Transportation Systems Center, U.S. Department of Transportation, *Benefit-Cost Evaluation of a Highway-Railroad Intermodal Control System (ICS)*, prepared for: Alstom, New York State Department of Transportation, Federal Highway Administration, *et al.*, (June, 2004).

Lord, Dominique, *et al.*, *Statistical Challenges with Modeling Motor Vehicle Crashes: Understanding the Implications of Alternative Approaches*, Center for Transportation Safety, Texas Transportation Institute, Texas A & M University (March 22, 2004).

Margiotta, Richard, Corporation, COMSIS and Science Applications International Corporation, *Incorporating Traffic Crash and Incident Information into the Highway Performance Monitoring System Analytical Process*, "Chapter 2," prepared for: Federal Highway Administration, (September, 1996).

Neale, Vicki L., *et al.*, National Highway Traffic Safety Administration, U.S. Department of Transportation, *An Overview of the 100-Car Naturalistic Study and Findings*, (Available at: www.nhtsa.dot.gov/staticfiles/DOT/NHTSA/NRD/Multimedia/PDFs/Crash%20Avoidance/Driver%20Distraction/100Car_ESV05summary.pdf).

Persaud, B.N., Canada Ministry of Transportation, *Roadway Safety: A Review of the Onario Experience and of Relevant Work Elsewhere*, (1992).

Report to Congress on the Large Truck Causation Study, Federal Motor Carrier Safety Administration, U.S. Department of Transportation, MC-R/MC-RRA (March, 2006).

Sabey, B.E., and G.C. Staughton, "Interacting roles of road environment, vehicle and road user in accidents," *Presented at: 5th International Conference on the International Association for Accident and Traffic Medicine*, London (1975).

"SafetyAnalyst," Available at: http://www.safetyanalyst.org (Last Accessed: November 18, 2004).

Treat, J.R., *et al.*, Indiana University, *Tri-level study of the causes of traffic accidents*, prepared for: U.S. Department of Transportation (1977).

Twomey, James M., *et al.*, Federal Highway Administration, U.S. Department of Transportation, *Interchanges*, Vol. IV of VI, *Safety Effectiveness of Highway Design Features*, FHWA/RD-91/047 (1992).

Vogt, A., and J.G. Bared, "Accident Models for Two-Lane Rural Segments and Intersection," *Transportation Research Record*, Transportation Research Board:1635 (1998).

Wang, J., *et al.*, Turner Fairbank Highway Research Center, Federal Highway Administration, U.S. Department of Transportation, *Safety Effects of Cross-Section Design for Rural, Four-Lane, Non-Freeway Highways*, FHWA-RD-98-071 (1998).

Zeeger, Charles V., and Forrest M. Council, Federal Highway Administration, U.S. Department of Transportation, *Cross Sections*, Vol. III of VI, *Safety Effectiveness of Highway Design Features*, FHWA/RD-91/046 (1992).

Zeeger, Charles V., *et al.*, Federal Highway Administration, U.S. Department of Transportation, *Pedestrians and Bicyclists*, Vol. VI of VI, *Safety Effectiveness of Highway Design Features*, FHWA/RD-91/049 (1992).

Zeeger, Charles V., *et al.*, Federal Highway Administration, U.S. Department of Transportation, *Alignment*, Vol. II of VI, *Safety Effectiveness of Highway Design Features*, FHWA/RD-91/045 (1992).

Appendix 1: The Draft 2nd-Order Model

This appendix contains output from the most complex version of the model later adopted. It contains additional variables and interaction effects left out of the recommended HERS model. Extra variables include speed limits and lane widths, both of which were dropped for a lack of firm causal relationships with crashes. Surface widths were also dropped because the effects of on-street parking, turning lanes, and other geometric determinants of surface length can not be disentangled. Moreover, HPMS does not contain surface width variables and so it could not be factored into HERS estimates. Other interaction effects were dropped from the model due to a lack of statistical significance and predictive power.

The output tables from this series of estimates is reproduced below. As can be seen by comparing Table 20 and Table 15, the estimates of the retained coefficients do not change much in the fuller model, indicating that the excess variables are not correlated with the retained ones. Using the sum of Pearson residuals as a measure, it appears that the reduced model actually has improved predictive power over the full one, though the difference is small. Similarly, other measures of goodness-of-fit do not change much, providing more evidence that the dropped variables add little to the model. With one exception, the graphs are virtually indistinguishable from those in the main text and so are not shown again here. The exception is for the marginal effects graphs, where the addition of variables containing higher order terms of grade degree transforms the line from linear into a curve.

Table 20. Comparison of 1st and 2nd Order Poisson and Negative Binomial Regressions (original second order)

	Poisson (1st)		NegBin (1st)			Poisson		NegBin	
	coef	se	coef	se		coef	se	coef	se
# Curves	0.017*	0.009	0.017**	0.009		-0.006	0.025	-0.014	0.028
Avg Curve Length (0.10 miles)	-0.388***	0.037	-0.358***	0.031		-0.398***	0.063	-0.394***	0.061
Avg Curge Degree	0.002**	0.001	0.004***	0.001		0.007*	0.004	0.003	0.005
# Grades	-0.047***	0.005	-0.041***	0.005		-0.104***	0.011	-0.095***	0.010
Avg Grade Length (0.10 miles)	-0.087***	0.015	-0.058***	0.015		-0.125***	0.019	-0.116***	0.017
% Grade	0.011**	0.005	0.002	0.006		0.018	0.014	0.017	0.015
# Intersections	0.023***	0.003	0.060***	0.003		0.065***	0.004	0.103***	0.005
%age Truck Traffic	-0.015***	0.002	-0.010***	0.002		-0.004	0.004	0.006	0.004
Lane Width	0.014	0.017	0.052***	0.015		-1.011	0.619	0.982	0.641
Surface Width	0.022***	0.001	0.021***	0.001		0.079***	0.007	0.077***	0.007
Shoulder Width	-0.061***	0.004	-0.048***	0.004		-0.101***	0.009	-0.080***	0.010
ln(MVMT)	0.831***	0.013	0.720***	0.011		0.839***	0.014	0.887***	0.014
# Curves^2						0.001	0.001	0.001	0.001
Avg Curve Length (0.10 miles)^2						0.039***	0.012	0.028**	0.011
Avg Curve Degree^2						-0.000	0.000	-0.000	0.000
# Grades^2						0.001**	0.000	0.001**	0.001
Avg Grade Length (0.10 miles)^2						0.001***	0.000	0.001***	0.000
Avg % Grade^2						-0.002	0.002	-0.002	0.002
# Intersections^2						-0.001***	0.000	-0.001*	0.000
%age Truck Traffic^2						-0.001***	0.000	-0.001***	0.000
Lane Width^2						0.042	0.028	-0.046	0.029
Surface Width^2						-0.001***	0.000	-0.001***	0.000
Shoulder Width^2						0.006***	0.001	0.005***	0.001
Avg Grade Length * Avg % Grade						0.016***	0.003	0.015***	0.003
Avg Curve Length * Avg Curve Degree						0.002	0.004	0.008	0.007
# Curves * # Intersections						0.000	0.001	0.001	0.002
# Grades * # Intersections						0.002***	0.001	0.003**	0.001
# Curves * # Grades						0.006***	0.002	0.009***	0.003
ln(MVMT) * # Curves						-0.013	0.010	-0.020	0.013
ln(MVMT) * # Grades						0.016***	0.006	0.008	0.006
ln(MVMT) * # Intersections						-0.020***	0.003	-0.046***	0.003
ln(MVMT)^2						0.074***	0.006	0.082***	0.006
Constant	0.903***	0.194	0.287*	0.164		5.966*	3.434	-5.419	3.534
ln(alpha)			-0.169***	0.020				-0.230***	0.019
significance stars: * 10%, ** 5%, *** 1%									

Table 21. Residuals Based on Predicted Crashes (original 2nd order)

	Poisson Difference	Poisson Pearson	NegBin Difference	NegBin Pearson
0	0.145	2,278.581	0.023	36.026
1	-0.033	108.179	-0.024	61.129
2	-0.046	278.665	-0.013	26.914
3	-0.033	204.888	-0.005	6.274
4	-0.021	121.875	-0.002	1.868
5	-0.008	26.128	0.004	6.846
6	-0.005	10.361	0.003	6.378
7	-0.004	9.911	0.001	1.251
8	-0.002	3.620	0.002	2.480
9	0.000	0.180	0.003	12.727
Sum	-0.008	3,042.387	-0.008	161.894

Table 22. Goodness-of-Fit Statistics (original 2nd Order)

	Poisson (1st Degree)	NegBin (1st Degree)	Poisson	NegBin
N	19942	19942	19942	19942
Log-Lik Intercept Only	-107,877.012	-48,926.354	-107,877.012	-48,926.354
Log-Lik Full Model	-58,444.722	-42,814.423	-56,872.380	-42,418.226
Deviation	116,889.443	85,628.845	113,744.759	84,836.452
df(Deviation)	19929	19928	19909	19908
LR	98,864.580	12,223.862	102,009.264	13,016.255
df(LR)	12	12	32	32
Prob > LR	0.000	0.000	0.000	0.000
McFadden's R2	0.458	0.125	0.473	0.133
McFadden's Adj R2	0.458	0.125	0.472	0.132
ML(Cox-Snell) R2	0.993	0.458	0.994	0.479
Cragg-Uhler(Nagelkerke) R2	0.993	0.462	0.994	0.483
AIC	5.863	4.295	5.707	4.258
AIC*n	116,915.443	85,656.845	113,810.759	84,904.452
BIC	-80,419.282	-111,669.980	-83,365.955	-112,264.361
BIC*n	-98,745.773	-12,105.055	-101,692.446	-12,699.437

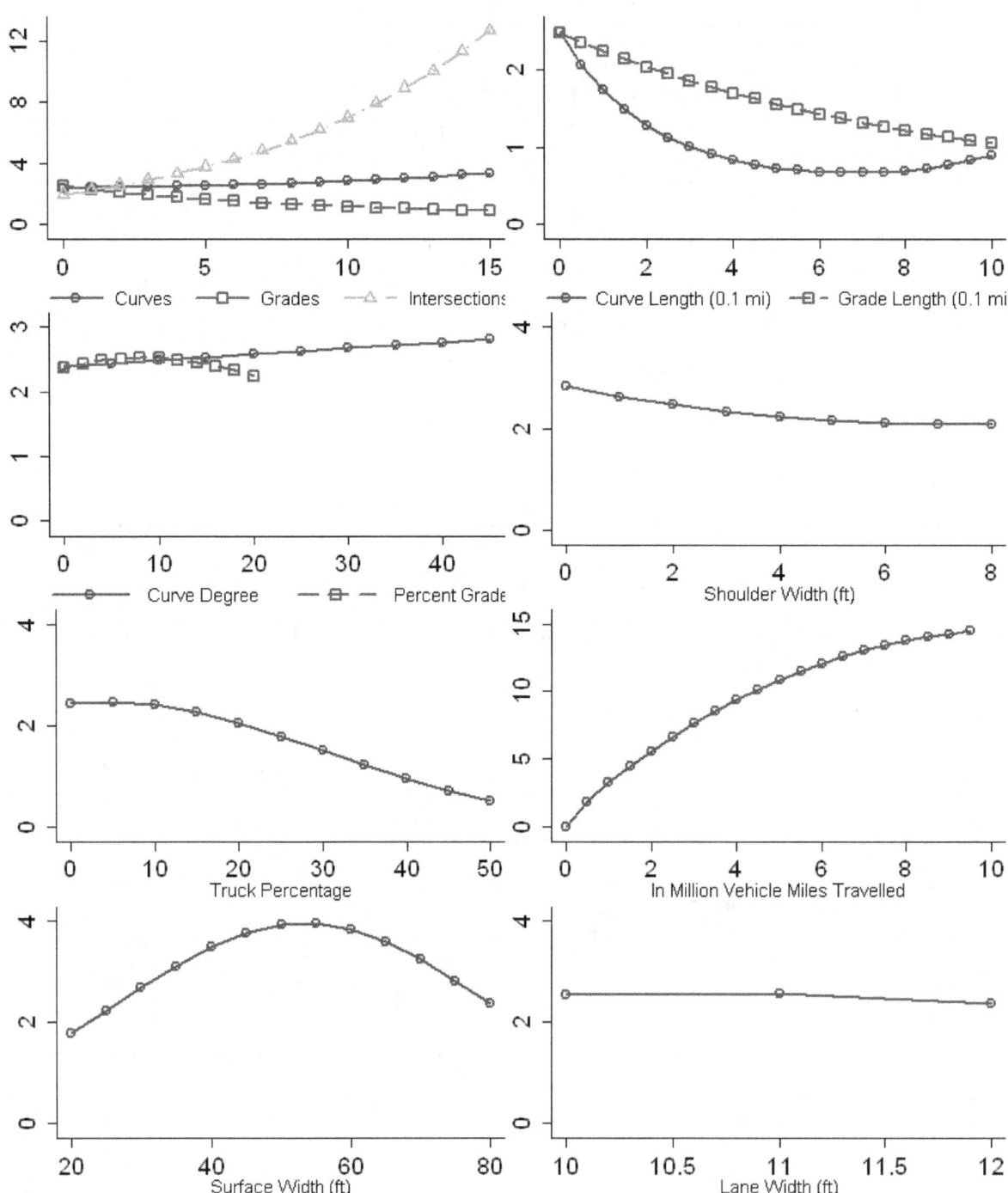

Figure 35. Predicted Crash Rates vs. Values of Explanatory Variables with all Other Variables Held at Mean (original 2nd order)

Appendix 2: State-level Statistics

This appendix contains summary statistics and correlation information for both Ohio and Washington individually. They are reproduced in Table 23 to Table 26.

Table 23. Ohio Summary Statistics

	mean	sd	min	25th	median	75th	max
# Crashes	5.827	10.080	0.000	0.000	2.000	7.000	191.000
# Curves	0.189	0.817	0.000	0.000	0.000	0.000	19.000
Avg Curve Length in 1/10th miles	0.049	0.206	0.000	0.000	0.000	0.000	3.500
Avg Curve Degree	1.669	8.789	0.000	0.000	0.000	0.000	96.000
# Grades	0.227	0.830	0.000	0.000	0.000	0.000	15.000
Avg Grade Length in 1/10th miles	0.137	0.542	0.000	0.000	0.000	0.000	18.300
Avg Percent Grade	0.633	1.871	0.000	0.000	0.000	0.000	18.000
# Intersections	3.159	3.680	0.000	1.000	2.000	4.000	37.000
Lane Width	11.653	0.699	10.000	12.000	12.000	12.000	12.000
Shoulder Width	3.064	3.068	0.000	0.000	3.000	5.000	15.000
Surface Width	27.874	7.809	16.000	24.000	24.000	33.000	77.000
Speed Limit	39.813	9.461	20.000	35.000	35.000	45.000	55.000
%age Truck Traffic	5.416	4.183	0.690	2.960	4.325	6.510	50.110
Million Vehicle Miles Travelled	1.417	2.012	0.000	0.302	0.705	1.681	22.884

Table 24. Washington Summary Statistics

	mean	sd	min	25th	median	75th	max
# Crashes	1.772	2.799	0.000	0.000	1.000	2.000	31.000
# Curves	0.377	1.085	0.000	0.000	0.000	0.000	28.000
Avg Curve Length in 1/10th miles	0.170	0.501	0.000	0.000	0.000	0.000	9.100
Avg Curve Degree	1.317	4.446	0.000	0.000	0.000	0.000	79.580
# Grades	1.223	2.402	0.000	0.000	0.000	1.000	31.000
Avg Grade Length in 1/10th miles	0.661	2.115	0.000	0.000	0.000	0.750	66.300
Avg Percent Grade	0.522	1.106	0.000	0.000	0.000	0.491	10.000
# Intersections	0.931	1.416	0.000	0.000	1.000	1.000	17.000
Lane Width	11.695	0.502	10.000	11.000	12.000	12.000	12.000
Shoulder Width	4.083	3.301	0.000	0.000	4.000	7.000	20.000
Surface Width	30.196	10.632	20.000	22.000	24.000	36.000	82.000
Speed Limit	39.835	9.331	25.000	35.000	40.000	50.000	60.000
%age Truck Traffic	6.110	5.871	0.000	0.000	6.000	10.000	40.000
Million Vehicle Miles Travelled	0.794	1.272	0.003	0.154	0.366	0.891	20.258

Table 25. Ohio Correlations

	# Crash	# Curves	Avg Curve Length	Avg Curve Degree	# Grades	Avg Grade Length	Avg % Grade	# I-sect	Lane Width	Shldr Width	Surf Width	Speed Limit	%age Truck Traffic	In MVMT
# Crashes	1.000													
# Curves	0.054	1.000												
Avg Curve Length	0.010	0.485	1.000											
Avg Curve Degree	-0.013	0.362	0.200	1.000										
# Grades	0.101	0.388	0.192	0.108	1.000									
Avg Grade Length	0.034	0.285	0.194	0.101	0.453	1.000								
Avg % Grade	0.032	0.314	0.202	0.130	0.696	0.705	1.000							
# Intersections	0.441	0.194	0.096	0.055	0.252	0.115	0.161	1.000						
Lane Width	0.080	-0.147	-0.063	-0.065	-0.113	-0.048	-0.111	-0.009	1.000					
Shoulder Width	-0.101	0.034	0.106	-0.020	0.039	0.037	0.032	-0.039	-0.125	1.000				
Surface Width	0.139	-0.150	-0.122	-0.051	-0.140	-0.091	-0.139	-0.018	0.470	-0.448	1.000			
Speed Limit	-0.108	0.144	0.169	0.021	0.137	0.112	0.112	-0.014	-0.160	0.426	-0.353	1.000		
%age Truck Traffic	-0.093	-0.050	-0.032	-0.025	-0.051	-0.034	-0.060	-0.069	0.071	0.142	-0.023	0.188	1.000	
In MVMT	0.662	0.146	0.100	-0.003	0.233	0.108	0.126	0.558	0.021	0.094	-0.070	0.085	-0.049	1.000

Table 26. Washington Correlations

	# Crash	# Curves	Avg Curve Length	Avg Curve Degree	# Grades	Avg Grade Length	Avg % Grade	# I-sect	Lane Width	Shldr Width	Surf Width	Speed Limit	%age Truck Traffic	ln MVMT
# Crashes	1.000													
# Curves	0.166	1.000												
Avg Curve Length	-0.004	0.317	1.000											
Avg Curve Degree	0.012	0.413	0.219	1.000										
# Grades	0.286	0.361	0.107	0.125	1.000									
Avg Grade Length	0.018	0.108	0.122	0.010	0.097	1.000								
Avg % Grade	0.042	0.152	0.120	0.129	0.274	0.189	1.000							
# Intersections	0.392	0.127	-0.024	0.022	0.353	-0.011	0.008	1.000						
Lane Width	-0.096	-0.112	-0.029	-0.065	-0.100	-0.032	-0.043	-0.039	1.000					
Shoulder Width	0.070	0.047	0.115	-0.041	0.034	0.079	-0.000	-0.062	-0.242	1.000				
Surface Width	-0.054	-0.152	-0.123	-0.042	-0.136	-0.102	-0.083	-0.003	0.483	-0.543	1.000			
Speed Limit	0.045	0.048	0.107	-0.115	0.072	0.097	-0.036	-0.144	-0.190	0.481	-0.382	1.000		
%age Truck Traffic	-0.051	-0.040	0.011	-0.096	-0.008	0.030	-0.040	-0.005	0.034	0.099	-0.056	0.180	1.000	
ln MVMT	0.535	0.314	0.156	0.007	0.519	0.105	0.080	0.319	-0.155	0.201	-0.239	0.257	-0.018	1.000

HERS   *Safety Model Assessment and Two-Lane Urban Crash Model*